Veteran Talking Machines

HISTORY AND COLLECTORS' GUIDE

MIDAS BOOKS

By the same author
Model Car Collecting
Veteran Sewing Machines
Fairs and Revels
Sports and Games—history and origins
The Working Travellers

In the same Midas Collectors' Library
Smoothing Irons
Scales and Balances (in preparation)
Stoneware Jars and Pots (in preparation)
Coin Operated Machines (in preparation)
Tinplate and Enamelled Signs (in preparation)
Motor Badges and Figureheads (in preparation)

First published 1977 by
MIDAS BOOKS
12 Dene Way, Speldhurst
Tunbridge Wells, Kent TN3 0NX

© Brian Jewell 1977

ISBN 0 85936 085 7 (CASED EDITION)
ISBN 0 87069 222 4 (PAPERBOUND EDITION—U.S.A. ONLY)

Printed in Great Britain
by Chapel River Press, Andover, Hampshire

CONTENTS

Edison Standard C

Text of words spoken on 'plates' of Berliner's gramophone issued by Parkins & Gotto, 60 Oxford Street, London W.1.

We don't want to fight,
But by jingo if we do;
We've got the ships, we've got the men,
We've got the money too.
We've fought the bear before,
But while we're Britons true,
The Russians shall not have Constantinople.
A b c d e f g h
One, two, three, four, five, six,
Seven, eight, nine, ten, eleven, twelve.

A healthy boy was Alfred Jones,
So fat you could not feel his bones,
His skin was sleek and smooth as silk
And his mother gave him bread and milk,
But he left it standing by his side,
And only blubbered, roared and cried,
I don't like bread and milk, I don't,
I won't eat bread and milk, I won't,
I hate the bread and milk, I do,
Oh! dear, Oh! dear, Boo-ooh-ooh-ooh.

Author's Note

The mark of a great invention is the effect it has on the lives, not only of those who see and use it as an innovation, but of future generations. There is no doubt that the talking machine is a great invention. Its stamp on social history of the past century can be likened to the motor-car, aeroplane, typewriter, radio, television and electric power.

With the huge record industry as it is today, geared to output of music by the million discs, to cater for the insatiable needs of pop-cultured buyers in every high street, the disc is synonymous with music. Yet the pioneers could not have foreseen the enormous potential of this application for their invention —the first machines were capable only of reproducing speech, and that rather poorly. It's a wonder that anyone persisted in developing the talking machine from what it was in the beginning—a fascinating and ingenious mechanical toy.

But developed it was, and it is fitting that after 100 years of practical talking machines we should look back on the early years. I need not offer an excuse for the fact that this book has been written, but feel perhaps an apology is needed for its limited scope. In the pages available it has been necessary to keep biographical references to a minimum and to give as much emphasis as possible to the machines themselves. But this is a book for collectors, particularly newcomers, and I hope that those who will be attracted to early talking machines in the centenary year will find some useful guidelines to identification and dating of instruments.

I wish the data could be more complete but so many instruments have been produced; this is a comparatively new field of historical research and there is much to learn.

The long standing enthusiasts will, I hope, bear with me through the pages of what to them will be elementary. But even the pundits may find something new.

B. J.

Tunbridge Wells, January 1977.

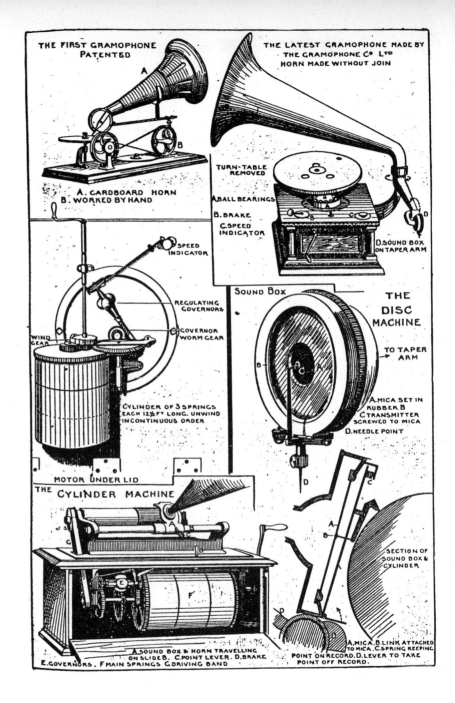

Illustration from Harmsworth Encyclopedia 1906

6

1. History: The Front Runners

Every invention calls for a date and the name of the founder of the feast. The sewing machine is attributed to Isaac Merritt Singer in 1851, the motor car to Gottlieb Daimler and Karl Benz in 1886, the typewriter to Christopher Latham Scholes in 1872, and wireless to Guglielmo Marconi in 1895. Everything needs its label so quiz masters can tease the minds of contestants. The trouble is that not one of these credits is true. In every case the basic principles of the invention had been well established years before.

Mention 'talking machines' and most people will respond, 'Thomas Alva Edison, 1877'. But it was some twenty years earlier that the sound reproduction machine made its debut in Paris. It was about 1855 that Debain conceived the design of the mechanical piano that would play music which had been previously recorded, probably inspired by the street or handle pianos which used small pins on the surface of a barrel to activate the string-striking hammers.

About the same time, also in France, Leon Scott de Martinville was working on an invention which he called the *phonautograph* (see Fig. 1). This was a machine for reproducing sound waves in line form. It could not reproduce sound but it was a foundation stone upon which later developments, particularly by Emile Berliner, were based. The phonautograph comprised a large horn at the narrow end of which was stretched a membrane. The stylus was fixed in the centre of this membrane. The other end of the stylus was in contact with a sheet of smoke blackened paper wrapped round a cylinder. When sound waves were introduced into the horn, while the cylinder was being rotated at a uniform rate, the stylus drew the waves of sound on the paper. The phonautograph was manufactured from 1859 by Konig, maker of acoustic instruments.

Next, chronologically in the story of the talking machine, came the Parisian Charles Cros, a remarkable man who crammed much into his brief life—he died at 46. He practised medicine, was a chemist, philosopher, poet and, of course, inventor. On 10 April 1877, Charles Cros walked into the Academie des Sciences and left a package of papers with the request that it should be opened on 3 December the same year. Whether or not Cros beat Edison, who first used his phonograph in July 1877, is a matter for conjecture. It is unlikely that Cros built a working model but it is obvious that he had the foundation of a practical machine. His idea was generally based on Leon Scott de Martinville's phonautograph in that a stylus attached to a diaphragm marked out a track on a smoke-blackened disc—note *disc* not cylinder as in the case of the phonautograph. Then by photographic process the track was to be reproduced in an engraved form on a disc of hard material. The disc could then be played back through the stylus, diaphragm and horn.

1   *Leon Scott's Phonautograph, 1857*

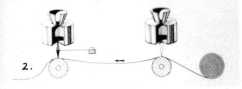

2.

There might have been a different history of the talking machine if Cros had been successful in his attempts to interest the prominent scientific instrument maker, Breguet, in the manufacturing of the machine. In the event the Cros invention joins the ranks of non-starters, with Thomas Saint's sewing machine of 1790, and Henry Mill's 'typewriter' of 1714.

So much for pre-history. We now come to that eventful day in July 1877 when 30-year old Thomas Alva Edison shouted 'hulloo' through the mouthpiece of his phonograph and then played it back. Edison was a professional inventor, running factories of inventions at Menlo Park and West Orange, New Jersey, for exploitation and sale to the ever hungry nineteenth century American industry. His credit sheet includes many developments in telegraphy, the megaphone, the kinetoscope, methods of electric lighting, power and traction. He had the honour, rare for inventors, of having his biography published before he was 50: *Dickson's Life and Inventions of T. A. Edison*.

Edison conceived the notions which he passed to other mechanics to bring them to practical form in the workshops. In the case of the phonograph, much of the credit must go to John Kruesi who actually built the first phonographs under Edison's direction.

It must not be thought that the conception of the phonograph was an accident, but the invention of a talking machine was not Edison's main consideration. He had been working on an instrument for telegraphy that would transcribe a Morse signal into marks on a rotating disc or strip. The 'record' was then to be used for relaying the message at a desired speed. (Fig. 2). During the course of these experiments he had the notion that if a diaphragm and a stylus were used, the sound waves of speech may be sufficient to indent a revolving strip of paraffin soaked paper, and if the so marked strip was drawn under a stylus fixed to a telephone earpiece, (Alexander Graham Bell's telephone was then being demonstrated at the Philadelphia Centennial Exhibition) the sound of the human voice might be reproduced.

A rough model was constructed and Edison heard his 'hulloo' come back to him in July 1877. Even then Edison was still thinking of relating the instrument to telegraphy. It was probably F. Johnson, one of Edison's associates at the West Orange workshops, who persuaded him to think in terms of talking machines. In early November 1877 Johnson was lecturing on telegraphy inventions in Buffalo and was greatly impressed by the reception of the news that the human voice could be reproduced. On 17 November a letter from Johnson, published in *The Scientific American*, stated that Edison was working on a phonograph using tinfoil instead of paraffin soaked paper. Within a few days John Kruesi had completed a prototype of this instrument and on 6 December Edison took it into the offices of *The Scientific American*, the editor of which wrote in the 22 December issue:

Mr Thomas A. Edison recently came into our office, placed a little machine on our desk, turned a crank, and the machine enquired as to our health, asked us how we liked the phonograph, informed us that it was very well, and bid us a cordial good-

2   Edison's Telephone Repeater, 1877

night. These remarks were not only perfectly audible to ourselves, but to a dozen or more persons gathered around.
(Fig. 3)

The first true phonograph comprised a 4ins diameter brass drum with a helical groove tooled on the circumference. The drum was mounted on a threaded axle, the rotation of which would move the drum laterally through $\frac{1}{10}$in—the same pitch as the groove. The tinfoil strip was wrapped round the drum and a stylus attached to a diaphragm and mouthpiece placed in contact with the strip. When a message had been recorded the mouthpiece was removed and a reproducer connected. This had a more sensitive diaphragm which reproduced the voice when the axle was rotated.

It must have been a good Christmas that year for Edison, Kruesi and Johnson.

During this important year in the history of the talking machine, 1877, other men who were later to make developments in this field were brought together. Emile Berliner, who had emigrated from Hanover to the United States seven years earlier, invented and patented a microphone, the manufacturing rights of which he sold to the Bell Telephone Company with whom he took up employment. But it was to be some three years in the case of the Bell concern, and ten years for Berliner, before their names were associated with talking machines.

On 24 April 1878, the Edison Speaking Phonograph Company was established at 203 Broadway, New York, its main role being the hiring of instruments together with quantities of blank tinfoil to travelling showmen, who charged for demonstrations and paid the Edison Company a percentage of the takings. It was at one of these performances that what is thought to be the first musical recording was made: a cornet solo of Yankee Doodle by one, Jules Levy. The company also marketed the Edison Parlour Speaking Phonograph at $10 per annum.

Meanwhile, news of the phonograph had come to England through Henry Edmunds who returned from an engineering study tour in the U.S.A. and on 17 January 1878 *The Times* published Edmund's article describing Edison's machines which he had seen demonstrated at a lecture. Now came an untypical piece of adventurous foresight on the part of a government official. William Preece, the Chief Engineer of the G.P.O. read the article and was so impressed that he immediately commissioned Edmunds to superintend the making of a tinfoil phonograph by Augustus Stroh, a post office engineer colleague of Preece. This Edmunds/Stroh phonograph was demonstrated as part of a lecture on the telephone given by Preece at the Royal Institution on 1 February. *The Graphic* reported:

Mr Preece explained how he had, with great difficulty, obtained this instrument, which was, he believed, the first to be exhibited in London. A gentleman [Edmunds] returned only a week before from America had kindly furnished him with drawings, and he had fortunately been able to enlist the services of the greatest mechanic of the day, who had, by working day and night, completed that afternoon the phonograph which stood before the audience. After remarking on the difficulty of knowing what

3 *Replica of Edison's Tinfoil Phonograph, 1877*

4   *W. H. Preece with Tinfoil Phonograph, 1878*

5   *Tinfoil Phonograph with Flywheel, 1878*

6   *Tinfoil Phonograph with Gravity Motor, 1878*

to say in the circumstances, Mr Preece spoke into the phonograph, 'Hey diddle diddle, the cat and the fiddle [nursery rhymes seem to feature a great deal in the history of talking machines—Edison's first trial record is said to have been 'Mary had a little Lamb'] and after waiting a minute or so the instrument was caused to repeat what he had said. The words were distinctly heard but the voice was very faint and an unearthly caricature. Professor Tyndall then made his way to the table and gave the phonograph a well-known quotation from the works of Tennyson, who was present, 'Come into the garden Maud,' which was afterwards echoed to the satisfaction of the audience. (See Fig. 4).

A further lecture, this time to the Society of Telegraph Engineers, was given by Preece on 27 February. On this occasion he had three machines to demonstrate:

A replica of Edison's December 1877 instrument built by an amateur mechanic, W. Pidgeon.

A phonograph sent from the U.S.A. by Edison, brought by his agent, Puskas. This was an improved model with a heavy flywheel and single diaphragm and stylus for both recording and reproduction.

The third driven by a clockwork motor powered by a falling weight was Stroh's second model. Like Edison's improved model, this machine used a single diaphragm and stylus. (Mr V. K. Chew of the London Science Museum considers that this motorised development signifies the fact that in England the phonograph was held to be a scientific instrument rather than a toy).

(See Figs. 5 and 6).

The London Stereoscopic Company—an illustrious name in the field of photography—opened negotiations with Edison to manufacture the phonograph in England. On 22 March (a month before the establishment of the Edison Speaking Phonograph Company in New York), London Stereoscopic received their indentures under which the tinfoil phonograph could be made. It is believed that Stroh was responsible for the design. By 1886 London Stereoscopic had three models on sale:

Hand-cranked without flywheel: £5.

With flywheel: £10 10s.

Falling weight motor driven: £25.

The company made phonographs—in the later years with wax cylinders—until 17 December 1891, when the Edison United Phonograph Company purchased back the indenture for £100 plus £1,000 for phonographs and parts in stock.

The U.S.A. and England were not the only places where phonographic development was taking place. In Paris, Le Phonographe Edison were producing the Hardy Tinfoil Phonograph under similar indentures to those granted by Edison to London Stereoscopic.

Mechanical drive at this time was by threaded axle, either crank-turned or activated by falling weight. An important breakthrough came in 1883 when London schoolmaster, J. E. Greenhill built a phonograph with a spring motor made by William Fitch and Son. This means of drive was to be used almost exclusively until the perfection of small mains powered electric motors.

Scottish born Alexander Graham Bell started to take an interest in talking machines at an early date. In 1879 his father-in-law was one of the main stockholders of the Edison Speaking Phonograph Company. But Bell waited until after winning the Prix Volta—a scientific award established by Napoleon III and administered by the French Government—before making active experiments. The year was 1880 and by this time American public interest in Edison's phonograph had begun to wane. Bell could see the reasons.

The tinfoil phonograph was undoubtedly a crude instrument, capable of reproducing only a distorted image of the speaker's voice. The recognisable recording of music was virtually impossible. Bell believed that better things could be achieved.

With money received from the French award, the Volta Laboratory Association was set up in Washington, DC, with the aim of experimenting in electro-acoustics. These experiments were put in the hands of two recruits: 27-year old Charles Sumner Tainter, and Bell's cousin, Chichester, then 33.

Steadily, although not confining their experiments to talking machines, the two men worked for four years, trying out all manner of recording surfaces, on cylinder, disc and tape, but generally using the basic principles of Edison's phonograph. The result, in 1885, was the wax cylinder *graphophone* which received its U.S. patent on 6 May 1886. (Fig. 7 8).

Meanwhile, in Europe competitive movements were afoot. In 1884 the Berlin company of Biedermann & Czarnikow was founded—this was an important manufacturer, later to produce such instruments as the Triumph and the Triumphon. Somewhat outside the terms of reference of this book, but still within the field of sound reproduction, is the polyphon perforated disc machine which was developed about this year by German Paul Lochmann and Englishman Elias Parr.

Bell and Tainter's graphophone was not available for commercial sale until June 1888, by which time another inventor had entered the lists. This was Emile Berliner who, as previously mentioned, had worked with Alexander Graham Bell in 1877. Berliner was a self-taught acoustics and electrical engineer and his work on sound reproduction was inspired, like Charles Cros before him, by Scott de Martinville's phonautograph of 1857—an example of which he would certainly have seen in the Smithsonian Institution.

Berliner first built a simple phonautograph and fixed the trace on the smoke-blackened paper with shellac. This he had transformed into an etched groove by photo-engraving process on a thin metal plate. The plate was wrapped round the cylinder and played back through the recording diaphragm. (Fig. 9).

Berliner decided to replace the cylinder by a disc of glass coated with a thin layer of lamp black and linseed oil. The recording stylus was applied to the underside of the disc so the scraped material would fall away from the surface

7.

8.

7   *L. S. Tainter with Graphophone*

8   *Bell and Tainter Graphophone, 1886*

11

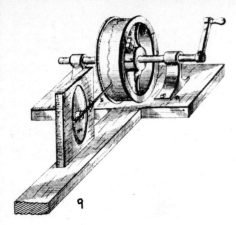

of the disc. The next stage in the development was to eliminate the photographic part of the operation. This was achieved by using a zinc plate coated with a solution of beeswax in benzine; there being left a thin layer of wax after the benzine had evaporated. The recording stylus cut a spiral in the wax, exposing the metal which was then etched with a solution of chomic acid.

Berliner called his machine the gramophone, a name that was to remain the property of his company until the rights were lost in a court action of 1909.

In the latter part of 1887 Emile Berliner was satisfied with the work on the development of his machine and applied for a U.S. Patent on 26 September. He demonstrated the gramophone to the Franklin Institute in Philadelphia on 16 May 1888 and then delayed exploitation until he had evolved a method of reproducing the zinc masters—a programme that was to take him into the following year.
(Fig. 10).

This then was the position in 1888. Thomas Edison, who had gone through a rather dull period since about 1880, when the public interest in the phonograph had begun to wane, renewed his enthusiasm and brought out the wax cylinder phonograph. Bell and Tainter had by now founded the Volta Graphophone Company to hold the patents and the American Graphophone Company to make and distribute the instruments. Berliner was happy with his process and was progressing with the reproduction of disc records.

The front runners were ready for the race and battle for commercial exploitation.

9 Berliner's Phonautograph, 1887
10 Berliner's Recording Machine, 1888

12

2. History: The Tangled Web

The year 1888 saw considerable activity, particularly in the U.S.A. On the scene came financier J. Lippincott who persuaded Thomas Edison to grant to him an exclusive agency in the U.S.A. for the exploitation of phonographs made by the Edison Phonograph Works. A similar agency was obtained from Bell and Tainter's American Graphophone Company whose production model was available from June of that year.

Lippincott's idea was this: to form a number of territorial companies under a parent organisation, the North American Phonograph Company. The subsidiaries were to hire, not sell, the instruments to commercial users as dictating machines. Unfortunately for Lippincott, there was a good deal of resistance to this kind of mechanisation among stenographers, and the North American Phonograph Company ran into trouble within a few years—but more about this later. (Fig. 11).

Both the phonograph and the graphophone were demonstrated at the British Association meeting held at Bath on 6 September 1888, the former being shown by Colonel Gourand, and the latter by Henry Edmunds whose enthusiasm for talking machines had not diminished over the past eleven years. (Fig. 12).

Basically, the two instruments were similar—the difference being in the cylinders: the phonograph used a thin coating of wax over a cardboard cylinder, whereas the graphophone cylinder was wholly of wax which could be shaved and reissued several times. The phonograph was fitted with a wet-cell battery electric drive.

A few months later, in the spring of 1889, at another demonstration—this time before the Elektrotechnische Verein in Germany—Emile Berliner showed his gramophone's worth in competition with Edison's phonograph. This resulted in the Walterhausen toy manufacturer, Kammerer and Reinhardt, contracting to build the instrument. So the 5ins rubber disc playing gramophone was first commercially available as a plaything. Manufacture of the instrument did not start in the U.S.A. for another four years. (Fig. 13).

Another German concern to start making talking machines about this time was A. Koltzow of Cologne.

In 1890 it was becoming obvious that the phonograph and graphophone did not have a particularly bright future as items of office machinery, and Lippincott's North American Phonograph Company was feeling the draught, if not a decidedly chilly wind. In an attempt to boost sales, Lippincott leaned towards the entertainment potential and issued what is acknowledged to be the first series of commercially available cylinder recordings which, by 1891,

11

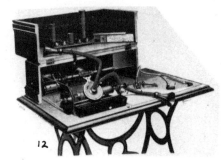

12

13

11   *Phonograph used by Stenographer*

12   *Graphophone on Treadle Base*

13   *Kammerer & Reinhardt, 1889*

13

14.

were being marketed by the Columbia Phonograph Company, one of the subsidiary companies that Lippincott had formed to hire out phonographs and graphophones. The first recording catalogue listed 194 titles.

In London in 1891 the Berliner-designed Kammerer & Reinhardt gramophone was being imported by Parkins & Gotto of Oxford Street. Another importer of the period was J. Lewis Young of 69 Fore Street, E.C.—a street perhaps better known as the home of several importers of German-made sewing machines. Young brought in American-made Edison instruments and continued to do so until 1893.

1892 saw the establishment of the London Phonograph Company by J. E. Hough who, apart from importing American-made machines, started to make cylinder records.

Things were beginning to become complicated for, in addition to Young and Hough and probably several others importing American products, there was the newly founded Edison Bell Phonograph Corporation Limited who purchased the British rights of the original Edison, and Bell and Tainter patents. Numerous court actions followed, but the independent importers continued to sell instruments as the American parent companies were not all that worried about who were buying.

The Edison Bell Phonograph Corporation Limited hired Drawing Room Phonographs at £10 per annum and commercial phonographs with recording facilities at the same rate. It is understood that some 700 machines were on hire.

In an attempt to introduce some order into the London situation, an agreement was eventually reached under which Hough held the right to sell phonographs for entertainment purposes while Edison Bell handled the business dictation machine application.

Augustus Stroh, who had been connected with talking machines since 1878, was by now manufacturing instruments in London, among them, it is believed, the Detective Disc Recording Machine. (Fig. 14). This had a clockwork motor which gave a slow speed recording of 20 minutes on a 5ins wax disc—it was this machine that was used to record a number of famous actors of the day.

1892 is also marked by the entry into manufacture by W. Bahre of Leipzig—one of the great names of German talking machine makers.

In 1893 the American Graphophone Company (Bell and Tainter) ceased production due, at least in part, to the top heavy reliance on selling the graphophone as a business machine. The Bell and Tainter patents were acquired by the Columbia Phonograph Company (Lippincott) of Washington, DC, which now began the actual production of graphophones. Edison saw in this action a threat to his control of his own patents, as he still had an agreement with Lippincott's North American Phonograph Company (the parent of Columbia) as an exclusive U.S. outlet. The sick North American Company was forced into liquidation through Edison's court actions to regain control of his patents. However, the scheme backfired and Edison found he was legally prevented from selling phonographs in the U.S.A. while the court proceedings lasted. One result of this restriction was that the Columbia Phonograph Company was able to market a spring-driven graphophone some two years before Edison was able to sell the Spring Driven Phonograph.

Emile Berliner at last started to make gramophones in America in 1893, forming the United States Gramophone Company at Washington, DC. A year later this company produced their first electrically driven machine.

The Berliner Gramophone Company was formed in 1896 to make instruments and 'plates' under licence from the parent, the United States Gramophone Company. But as yet the gramophone lacked the spring motor drive of its competitors, the phonograph and the graphophone.

An enterprising French engineer, Henri J. Lioret, devised what was probably the first novelty talking machine—a small mechanism that fitted inside a doll. Lioret called this doll Bebe Jumeau. The first, made in 1895, was delivered to the daughter of Czar Nicholas II of Russia. Bebe Jumeau appeared in Lioret's catalogue, together with other Lioretgraph instruments, until 1900. In London, Lioret was represented by Rowe & Company, 15 Aldermanbury Street. It is interesting to compare this doll with the Mae Starr doll manufactured in the U.S.A. in the 1930s. (Figs. 15 and 16).

In 1896 the Berliner Gramophone Company introduced their first spring motor instrument—the Baby Grand Gramophone. The motor was designed and built by Eldridge R. Johnson.

Adding to the confusion, the National Gramophone Company was established in New York by F. Seaman as an exclusive selling agency for the Berliner Gramophone Company. So, in this year, there were the National Gramophone Company (selling Berliner Gramophones), the National Phonograph Company (selling Edison Phonographs), and the Columbia Phonograph Company (selling Bell and Tainter patented graphophones).

It must be said that the gramophones did not offer very good sound reproduction, but they were comparatively inexpensive. The discs were cheaper to produce than cylinders, a fact that the American Graphophone Company (making Columbia/Bell and Tainter products) were beginning to realise. It was something which Edison refused to recognise and it was not until 1912 that the National Phonograph Company entered the disc market.

During the year 1896 Pathe Freres in Paris started recording operatic discs. In Berlin, Carl Lindstrom began making talking machines. An able business man, Lindstrom was to acquire many marques and labels over the next seventeen years as well as his own badge of Parlaphone. Lindstrom was one of several manufacturers to make the cheap but classic Puck type instrument —other makers of the Puck included Lyra and Fritz Puppel. Puck machines sold at the absurdly low price of between 3s 6d and 5s and in the U.S.A. they suffered the indignity of being given away free with Columbia cylinders.

The Berliner Gramophone Company in 1897 produced discs made from a

15.

16.

15 Lioret Doll, 'Bebe Jumeau'

16 'Mae Starr' Talking Doll

15

17.

plastic material called Durinoid—a shellac-based material that had hitherto been used only in the manufacture of buttons.

One of Berliner's employees in the Philadelphia works, J. Jones, filed a patent application covering a process for stamping discs. It took four years for the patent to be granted when it was immediately snapped up by the American Graphophone Company (Columbia/Bell and Tainter)—the web was beginning to get tangled.

Emile Berliner sent W. B. Owen to England with the brief to set up the Gramophone Company in London—with this franchise went the rights to sell instruments and recordings throughout Europe. Also in 1897, the National Phonograph Company (Edison) established its European headquarters—this time in Antwerp—and the Columbia Phonograph Company opened its Paris office to control operations on this side of the Atlantic.

The scene in London was gaining its own complexity. J. E. Hough, who had built up the London Phonograph Company in about 1892, now established Edisonia Limited, making instruments and records from masters he had acquired in the U.S.A. The Edison Bell Phonograph Corporation Limited, which held both Edison and Bell and Tainter British patent rights, was not in a healthy state and, in 1898, they were pleased to amalgamate with Hough, the man they had often faced across courtroom floors. The result of this merger was the Edison Bell Consolidated Phonograph Company with Hough as managing director. He also kept control of Edisonia Limited for the production of Popular, Ebony, Indestructible, and Grand Concert records.

Later in the year, Fred W. Gaisberg came over from the U.S.A. to join W. B. Owen at the Gramophone Company's Maiden Lane, Strand, headquarters. Gaisberg's commission was to manage the recording policy of the company and he has the distinction of being the pianist on the company's first London recorded disc. The actual record production was carried on at Hanover where Joseph Berliner—Emile's brother—was in control.

1898 saw some unusual design developments. A magnetic wire recorder was patented by Valdemar Poulsen while working with the Copenhagen Telephone Company. The Telegraphone, as it was called, was demonstrated at the 1900 Paris Exposition and later went into production at Springfield, Mass., U.S.A. (Fig. 17).

Another innovation of the year was made by the Polyphon Company of Chicago, a subsidiary of Carl Lindstrom's empire. This was an amplifier attachment with two soundboxes in tandem, each with its own horn.

If for nothing else, 1898 should be remembered as the year that Horace Short—later to be recognised as one of the famous aircraft manufacturing brothers—began experimenting with compressed air as a means of amplification. There was nothing really new in the idea; Edison had tried it years earlier and had abandoned the method. However, Short persisted and two years later, in 1900, he effectively demonstrated his invention from the top of the Eiffel Tower. Short gave up his acoustic work in favour of aviation in 1903 and sold

17   Poulsen's Telegraphone, 1898

16

the patent rights of the compressed air amplifier to Charles (later Sir Charles) Parsons, who improved on the concept, which was marketed from 1904 as the Auxetophone by what was by then Gramophone & Typewriter Limited.

The 1890s, looked at in retrospect, were a simmering cauldron as far as the talking machine industry was concerned. The crisis came in 1899 when, in the words of Mr V. K. Chew (*Talking Machines*—Science Museum Book, 1967), 'there followed a commercial battle as complex as it was ruthless'. To chart a track through the entwined jungle of that year would take a volume all to itself, and the best that can be achieved with this limited canvas is to mention some of the events which were to leave their marks on future years.

It will be recalled that in 1896 F. Seaman established the National Gramophone Company, New York, as a sales agency for the Berliner Gramophone Company, Philadelphia. Now, in 1899, Seaman, for reasons which are far from obvious, broke away from Berliner and set up the Universal Talking Machine Company for the purpose of producing the Zonophone. This was done in association with the American Graphophone Company (Columbia/Bell and Tainter). The Zonophone was an instrument which was identical to Berliner's gramophone. Production of the original gramophone was halted, but Eldridge Johnson—who had made the spring motor for the gramophone—formed another company (the Consolidated Talking Machine Company) to make the gramophone. In partnership with Berliner, the Victor Talking Machine Company was founded to make the Victor. This was in all respects the gramophone, but the name could not be used because of Registration laws.

There now emerged some recording process difficulties. To quote V. K. Chew: 'Johnson was by now using a process in which the recording was carried out, not by the etched plate method, but by incising a groove of constant depth in the surface of a thick wax blank. The recorded surface was then rendered electrically conducting and the metallic negative was deposited on it by electrolysis. This negative was then used for stamping the records, using now the shellac-based material that had been introduced in 1897.'

To explain the difficulties we have to go out of chronological order. J. Jones (who was working for Berliner) filed a patent application in 1897 that took four years in the granting. As mentioned before, the manufacturing rights of the patent were bought by the American Graphophone Company, who by 1902 were making the Disc Graphophone.

There was a situation that can only be described as chaotic, with Victor clashing with Jones, Berliner and American Graphophone patents. It was a legal bonanza in which the only people who could benefit were the lawyers. There had to be some sort of out-of-court agreement—and this was reached in 1902—under which the National Phonograph Company (Edison) made only cylinder machines, the Victor Talking Machine Company (Johnson and Berliner) produced only disc-playing instruments, and the Columbia Phonograph Company (Bell and Tainter) marketed both kinds—the actual manufacturer being the American Graphophone Company.

Let us return to 1899 for some light relief. One day in that year in the Maiden Lane premises of the Gramophone Company, W. B. Owen was attending to whatever business a talking machine manufacturer did in those days, when in walked Francis Barraud, an artist, wanting to borrow a brass horn to use as a model to up-date a picture he had painted a few years earlier. This was of a fox terrier sitting beside an Edison phonograph. Owen was impressed by Barraud's work and offered to buy the picture on condition that a gramophone was substituted for the phonograph. At that time the gramophone carried the 'Recording Angel' as a regular trade mark. It was not Owen, but Eldridge Johnson in the States (Victor Talking Machine Company) who first saw a trade mark potential in the Barraud painting, 'His Master's Voice' or 'Nipper', and it was used on U.S. made instruments and disc labels from an early date. In England, although given a limited showing on products, it was not widely used on records until 1909. When, in 1910, the Gramophone Company lost the exclusive right to use the word 'gramophone', it was decided to exploit 'His Master's Voice' to the full, both in pictures and words. (Fig. 18).

The National Phonograph Company (Edison) in 1899, introduced their 'Gem'—now a collector's classic—which could play two cylinders at one winding. In England, the 'Gem' was made by the Edison Bell Consolidated Phonograph Company (J. E. Hough) from 1904.

After 1900 came an amazing array of German-made machines that complicates the collector's and historian's comprehension still more. Excelsior in Nippes, Germany, (founded 1899) produced instruments based on Columbia (Bell and Tainter) designs. Their main sales outlets were through W. Bahre and the Holzweissig Company of Leipzig, and Murdoch in London.

The twentieth century came in with the talking machine industry in an expanding but confused state. There was no doubt that reproduced music was here to stay and makers had sufficient confidence to offer instruments at prices starting from a few shillings.

18   Gramophone with 'Nipper' model

LIST OF PLATES NOW READY

FOR THE

"GRAMOPHONE."

RECITATIONS.
17. Proverbs
18. Father William
20. Old King Cole
23. Manfred (*Byron*)
25. Lord's Prayer
26. Twinkle, Little Star
27. Thou knowest my pretty damsel
28. Morning Hymn
29. Jack and Jill
30. Mary had a Little Lamb
31. A Healthy Boy was Alfred Jones
32. Tom, he was a Piper
33. Simple Simon
34. My name is the 'Gramophone'
35. Cock Robin
36. Sing a Song of Sixpence
37. Old Mother Hubbard
38. Nursery Rhymes

SONGS.—ENGLISH.
40. We don't want to fight
41. For you, for you, my Darling
42. Auld Lang Syne
44. My Grandfather's Clock
48. Rule Britannia
50. Blue Bells of Scotland
53. Ta ra ra Boom-de-Ay
54. Knock'd 'em in the Old Kent Road
56. Long, long ago

FRENCH.
164. Père Victoire
165. La Boiteuse

GERMAN.
52. Kühlengrund
53. Wacht am Rhein
54. Rheinlied
61. Der Gute Kamerad
64. Soldatenlied
72. Deutschland über Alles

BRASS INSTRUMENTS.
75. Quintet (March)—Gruss aus Kiel
77. Quintet—Hohenfriedberger
78. „ Gasparone
81. „ Zu Augsburg
88. „ God save the Queen
111. Piston Solo—Deutschland
112. „ „ The Mail
606. Concert Piece
609. Mikado
113. Bugle Calls
116. Trombone Solo—Drinking
376. Quintet—Alte Dessauer

PIANO.
121. Bierwaltzer
122. Prophet's March

ASSORTED PLATES.
45. Farmyard Imitations (Animal Voices, &c.
120. Banjo Duet—Boccacio
130. Clarionette Solo, with variations
600. Old-fashioned Street Organ
650. Roll of Drums

The **Gramophone**

. . . AND . . .

HOW TO

USE IT.

PRICE OF PLATES, **1/-** EACH.

PARKINS & GOTTO, CO, OXFORD STREET, W.

The Gramophone ..

and How to Use it.

THE principal parts of the Gramophone are as follows :—

1. The Spring Motor, which furnishes the power to revolve the records. This is contained in a square wooden case, which it is not necessary to open, as the motor never requires oiling, and, with the exception of winding and regulating the speed, has only to be let alone.

2. Wooden arm or traveller, which carries the sound box and horn.

3. Sound Box.

4. The Horn.

5. The Needle Point.

6. Winding Key.

7. The Disc.

Directions for Use.

Unpack the Gramophone carefully from the packing case, and be careful not to overlook anything packed in the horn.

The contents of the case are as follows :—

1. Spring motor, with turntable and nickel-plated arm.

2. Wooden arm or traveller.

3. Sound box.

4. Horn.

5. Package of needles.

6. Winding key.

7. Discs ordered.

Place the motor case so that the nickel-plated arm will be at your right hand, the winding key will then be on your left. Place the wooden travelling arm in position by placing the pin with which it is provided into the socket of the nickle-plated arm. Take the sound box out of the little box into which it is packed and place the shaft into the nickel spring holder at the opposite end of the wooden arm, so that the sound box will be towards you on the inside of the arm. Turn the sound box in the holder until the projecting pin rests against the nickel-plate on the upper side of the wooden arm. Rest the large end of the horn on the wire support attached to the stationary end of the wooden arm, and connect the small end or elbow with the shaft of the sound box, which protrudes through the holder.

Insert a needle point under the thumb-screw of the sound box, and turn screw till fast. Then place the travelling end of the wooden arm so that it will lie in the rest at the back of the motor case, where it should always be kept when not in operation. Select a record disc, and, unscrewing the circular clamp from the central pivot in the turntable, place the disc, with the etched side up, upon the table and make secure by screwing the clamp down over it.

Apply the key to the winding apparatus at the left of the motor case and wind carefully as far as possible. (Do this after each selection to obtain the best results.)

Take the travelling end of the wooden arm from its resting-place and put it carefully in position, so that the needle point rests in the etched circle nearest to the outside edge of the disc, on the side next to the brake.

All being now ready, loosen the brake which holds the turntable. When the selection is finished, return travelling end of the wooden arm to its rest, being careful not to drop it or allow it to fall or remain at the front of the motor case.

General Instructions.

The speed of the turntable is regulated by a stop found on the left of the motor case and which can be turned with the fingers. The rate of speed can be determined by placing a slip of white paper under the clamp and counting the number of times it goes round in a minute. The faster it goes the higher the pitch.

T H E
GRAMOPHONE,
OR
Speaking Machine.

Emile Berliner's Patent.

PRICE TWO GUINEAS NETT, WITH SIX PLATES.

Extract from "The Queen."

"One funny curiosity, evidently based on the principles of the Phonograph, should cause endless amusement to children of all ages. We refer to the 'Gramophone,' or Speaking Machine, which can be taught to say almost anything, from pieces of verse to farmyard imitations. It is not claimed to be a scientific apparatus, though it will reproduce the human voice or other sounds of any kind as often as desired. **We had the pleasure of hearing one recite 'Twinkle, twinkle, little star,' in tones so absurd, that it was impossible not to laugh. It would prove an excellent antidote to a rainy day in the nursery.'**

The GRAMOPHONE.

Is an Apparatus for reproducing the human voice or other sounds of any kind, as often as desired. It reproduces the sounds so loudly that a hundred persons can hear them at the same time.

The **GRAMOPHONE** bears *no* resemblance in a scientific aspect to the Phonograph or the Graphophone.

Those having a **GRAMOPHONE** may buy an assortment of Plates —comprising recitations, songs, chorus and instrumental solos or orchestral pieces of great variety.

Collections of Plates become very valuable, and whole evenings may be spent going through a long list of interesting performances.

The **GRAMOPHONE** is intended and expected to be for the voice what photography is for the features, *i.e.* to secure an accurate and lasting record of voices.

INSTRUCTIONS FOR FITTING UP THE
GRAMOPHONE.

Place the base of the machine on a table with the wooden handle of the wheel towards you. After this, take the turn-table and put it into the column and oil all the frictional parts, and see that they are free from all dust. The armature on which the Diaphragm box is fixed can now be dropped into pillar. Place the needle in set screw so that it projects about a quarter of an inch from the screw. After this, put the funnel on to the piece of brass tube that projects from the Diaphragm box, and let the wide part of the funnel rest on the holder above the pivot. Put disc on the turntable and fix the same tightly. Place needle on the outside edge of disc and turn the handle of the machine at the rate of 150 turns to the minute. Be sure and see that the plate runs in a circle and is not out of the centre. Always turn the handle to the right, be sure and not turn it the wrong way. One needle will last for the performances of about 24 Plate. Never use the same needle over again without sharpening it, if so, it destroys the plate, The sound produced from the machine is the same as the human voice speaking through a trumpet. If you want to hear a more natural voice, fix the india-rubber tubes to the end of brass connector of the Diaphragm, and place the two glass tubes, one in each ear ; if the sound seems scratchy, place a little wadding or cotton wool in the wide end of the rubber tube. If you wish the machine to speak across a large hall you can get a trumpet made of tin, three times the length of the present one, by any ordinary tinman. The Diaphragm and Record Discs are the main parts of the machine. See that the spring of the Diaphragm box does not rest tightly against the side of same, as this is effected by temperature. If the Diaphragm box is taken out of the armature it must be put back again exactly the same, so that the needle stands 45 degrees towards the centre of the table.

3. History: Consolidation

As if W. B. Owen and the Gramophone Company Limited in London had not enough to do, making and selling talking machines and recording on discs, they took upon themselves the distribution of another kind of machine in 1900. Frank Lambert of Brooklyn, New York, is said to have taken seventeen years to perfect his typewriter. It was an ingenious machine which captured Owen's imagination. Accordingly, he acquired the European selling rights and reformed the Gramophone Company into Gramophone & Typewriter Limited, distributing also in France and Germany. It was claimed that speeds of 110 words per minute could be achieved with the Lambert—this is doubtful—and the machine sold well for a few years. However, in the face of ever-increasing competition the demand dropped and Owen abandoned the typewriter side of the business in 1907.

The Columbia Phonograph Company (Bell & Tainter) set up a sales office in London—hitherto their products had been distributed mainly by J. E. Hough's London Phonograph Company, Edisonia Limited and Edison Bell Consolidated Phonograph Company. Later in the year 1900, Columbia moved their European headquarters from Paris to London and, at about the same time, introduced their High Speed or Type XP cylinders. At the 1900 Paris Exposition, Columbia displayed the Multiplex Grand—a cylinder instrument with three soundboxes, each with its own horn—intended to play trio parts on three separate tracks. (Fig. 19).

Another strange invention to arrive in that year was covered by a British patent granted to T. B. Lambert. This was for a phonograph 'wired up and started to reproduce sound by means of independent movement such as the opening of a door'. In the next few years there were a number of phonographs designed for giving out advertising slogans when shop doors were opened, including one for Blue Band Margarine. (Fig. 20).

Barnett Samuel was a well-established musical instrument dealer when, in 1901, he turned his attention to talking machines. Within a short while Samuel was stocking most marques and was marketing his own—probably assembled from continental components—which he called the Dulcephone. Later Samuel was to introduce the world's first true portable, the Decca, and to found the company of that name.

The Columbia Phonograph Company (Bell and Tainter) took an important step in 1902 when they introduced the Type AJ—known as the Disc Graphophone—their first breakaway from cylinder-playing machines.

Meanwhile, at the Victor Talking Machine Company (Berliner/Johnson), Jones and Gibson were working hard on the development of what was to be known as the 'Exhibition' soundbox, destined to be fitted to almost all instru-

19 *Columbia Multiplex Grand, 1900*

20 *Blue Band Margarine Advertising Machine*

21.

22

ments of the Victor and Gramophone companies between 1905 and 1919. Until the outbreak of World War I it is believed that all these soundboxes were made at the Victor works in the U.S.A. After that time, all those fitted to the British-made instruments were made at the Hayes factory and marked 'His Master's Voice'.

The prize for the fun machine of the year 1902 must go to Stollwerk in Germany, who produced a toy machine—the unusual thing about it is that it played discs which were not thrown away when worn out—they were made from chocolate! (Fig. 21).

Pathe Freres opened their London sales office in 1903, marketing among other machines in their range, the Coq (£2 12s 6d) and the No. 0 Democrat (£1 1s).

The European rights of the International Zonophone Company (F. Seaman's successor to the Universal Talking Machine Company) were acquired by Gramophone & Typewriter Limited in London, and the British Zonophone Company was registered, managed for about a year by Charles (later Sir Charles) Sterling, who came to England from the U.S.A. in 1903 for this purpose. Sterling then moved to the Russell Hunting Record Company to control the making of Sterling cylinders. This was followed by a period of making Rena records, and when this concern was bought by the Columbia Company in 1909, Sterling became managing director of the British branch, and later, European general manager. 'Zonophone' survived as a 'badge label' on some machines made by Gramophone & Typewriter Limited.

The Edison Bell Consolidated Phonograph Company (J. E. Hough) opened a factory at Peckham, South East London in 1903, to make the Gold Moulded series of records as well as instruments.

Some weird and wonderful cabinet shapes appeared about this time, notably Hymnophon instruments built by Holweissig in Leipzig, the styles of the cabinets varying from beer barrels to grottoes. (Fig. 22).

1904 was the year of the introduction of the 'Morning Glory' horn. If there is one industrial product to typify the Edwardian drawing room it is this. Originally, it was sold by Gramophone & Typewriter as an optional extra. A year later it was fitted to the Melba instruments, and later to all models as standard. (Fig. 23).

The European headquarters of Edison's National Phonograph Company were moved from Antwerp to London, thus centring in Britain the European activities of all the main American companies.

The great St Louis Exhibition was opened in 1904 and one machine that could be seen at St Louis was the Columbia Quadruple Disc Graphophone, a wondrous machine equipped with four turntables mounted on a vertical shaft, each with its own horn. (Fig. 24).

Another gigantic instrument to be demonstrated that year was the Victor Triplephone at the Crystal Palace in London, in front of an audience of 20,000.

The Neophone Company of Finsbury Square, London, was established in

21   Stollwerk, 1905

22   Hymnophon Fass-Automat, 1909

24

1904, making phono-cut records with a white celluloid surface on a paper backing. These were 20ins diameter discs that played for 12 minutes—their most unusual feature was that the needle started near the centre of the disc and worked outwards.

This may be an appropriate moment to define the two types of records: phono-cut or 'hill and dale' records depend on an up and down movement of the stylus, whereas needle-cut records cause a sideways or lateral movement of the stylus.

In 1905, the Columbia Company in England established a factory at Wandsworth to make cylinders and discs. It coincided with the introduction of the Twentieth Century Premier Graphophone and the Columbia Sovereign—instruments intended to play 6ins Premier cylinders, the first products from the new Wandsworth works.

It will be recalled that back in 1888 Lippincott's North American Phonograph company was founded with the express purpose of exploiting talking machines for office use but, because of the resistance of stenographers, the venture was not a success. Now eighteen years later—in 1906—the resistance and interest had been worn down. Edison introduced the Business Phonograph and, in the same year, the Edison cylinders were slightly increased in length and the price reduced from 1s 6d to 1s.

Although Edison was at one time remaining steadfastly to cylinders, other manufacturers were not. Pathe Freres for instance, abandoned their cylinder production in 1906. Instruments were becoming more elegant in design. Gramophone & Typewriter Limited introduced the Sheraton, a styled cabinet model priced at £35, the features of which included a 12ins turntable and speed indicator.

1907 was an important year for the three American-born companies. Columbia commissioned Marconi as a technical adviser, using his name as a label marque. The company also brought out in this year a model they called the Grand Symphony—it was Columbia's first concealed horn model and was styled in the design of an upright piano!

Another internal horn machine which appeared this year was the Gramophone Grand—known in the U.S.A. as the Victor Victoria. Indeed, 1907 was a landmark year for Gramophone & Typewriter Limited. They finally decided to drop the sales of the Lambert typewriter and revert to the old name of the Gramophone Company Limited. A new factory was built at Hayes which, in addition to instruments, was to produce records which had hitherto been mainly manufactured at the Joseph Berliner managed Hanover works. To this day the Hayes factory is the main production unit of Electrical & Musical Industries.

The National Phonograph Company (Edison) was not to be left out of this year of innovation, producing as it did an AC electric mains supply instrument called the Alva—after the company's founder.

There was a growing battle for sales in the record field. In 1908 the National

23   *The Melba*

24   *Columbia Quadruple Disc Graphophone, 1904*

Phonograph Company introduced Amberol cylinders, which having twice as many grooves to the inch, played for four minutes instead of two. Conversion kits for existing instruments were marketed.

The Columbia Phonograph Company brought out 4½ins Blue Ribbon cylinders, as well as introducing the Dictaphone instrument on which Premier cylinders were played.

Not to be outdone, Hough's Edison Bell Consolidated Phonograph Company introduced three new series of records: Bell, which were double-sided 10½ins discs selling at 2s 6d, New Premier (N.P.) records and Phondisc in two sizes—12ins at 4s, and 8¾ins at 1s 6d. An instrument brought out by Edison Bell was the Discaphone, designed to play both needle-cut and phon-cut discs. This year, 1908, was the last for both Edisonia Limited and the Edison Bell Consolidated Phonograph Company. Both had been under the effective control of Hough since 1898 but now they became completely merged and, logically, were given the new name of J. E. Hough Limited.

Following the example of the Gramophone and Columbia companies in bringing out enclosed horn instruments, Edison's National Phonograph Company offered the Amberola range in 1909—a marque that was to continue in the catalogue for twenty years.

Edison's cylinders were among the few to survive World War I. So, too, were the 4minute playing cylinders made by the Indestructible Record Company of Albany, New York—a company taken over in 1909 by the Columbia Phonograph Company.

The 'Sheraton Gramophone Grand of 1907, in its elegant cabinet, had been an outstanding success and by 1909 the Gramophone Company Limited catalogued seven styles of Gramophone Grands with names like 'Chippendale' and 'Queen Anne'. In this year they also produced the Pigmy Grand with the Exhibition soundbox—the first of the company's portables. Initially it was sold without a lid, but this was added in 1910.

The Columbia Phonograph Company produced the last of their cylinder models in 1910. Cylinder records continued to be made by the company for another two years.

A number of devices were invented in the early years of the twentieth century which, when combined with a clock mechanism, would speak the time. One such invention, built in 1911, was that of B. Hiller, Berlin. The early instruments employed a perforated celluloid film, but by 1914 Hiller was using a conventional recording disc. It is understood that some 300 Hiller speaking clocks were built. Since the 1890s German manufacturers had been increasingly active in talking machine manufacture. One of the most prominent was Carl Lindstrom of Berlin who, by 1913, was in control of many German marques including Dacapo, Favorite, Fonotipia, Homophone, Jumbo, Beka, Lyrophon and Odeon, as well as Parlaphone which Lindstrom had founded.

The year 1913 brought a sign of things to come when Professor Lee de Forrest used a magnetic wire recorder for experiments in talking-film-making

The
Monarch
Gramophone.

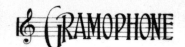

The
Monarch Senior
Gramophone.

Price, £7. 10.

Also in Mahogany, £8. 15

The Bijou Grand
(Mahogany).

Price, £30.

The
Gramophone Grand
(Sheraton Style).

Price, £52. 10.

Price, £11.

Also in Mahogany, £12. 10.

The Bijou Grand
. (Oak).

Price, £25.

*Gramophone Company Limited advertisement of
1908*

27

at the Biograph Studios, New York.

In 1913 Barnett Samuel & Sons Limited of London produced the first true portable machine, the Decca. It was destined to be the standard item of entertainment equipment in the British trenches of Flanders in World War I. In the words of immediate post-war sales literature:

WHAT DID YOU DO IN THE GREAT WAR—'DECCA'?

I was 'Mirth-Maker-in-Chief to His Majesty's Forces'; my role being to give our Soldiers and our Sailors music wherever they should be. In that capacity I saw service on every Front—France, Belgium, Egypt, Palestine, Italy and the Dardenelles; right in the Front Line and away back in Camps and Hospitals. All told, there were 100,000 'Deccas' on Active Service from start to finish of the War.

And, now that the War is over, I still pursue my calling but under pleasanter conditions . . .

The main innovation brought by the Decca was the way the tonearm opened into a metal shell in the raised lid. (Fig. 25).

In 1923 the Columbia Phonograph Company of Washington, DC, was bought out by its London-based European subsidiary. Probably more than most, the talking machine industry has always shown itself open to international exchanges of financial control and personnel throughout its history.

A Frenchman by the name of Louis Lumiere was granted a British patent in 1909, covering a pleated and varnished paper diaphragm to be used in place of a conventional soundbox, tone arm and horn. The patent rights were purchased by the Gramophone Company in London but application of the diaphragm to production instruments had to wait until the mid-1920s. Several Gramophone models of the 1924-7 period were fitted with 16ins diameter Lumiere diaphragms. In addition, the Sterling Primex, produced in 1923, by the Sterling Telephone & Electric Company, employed a Lumiere diaphragm made under Licence from the Gramophone Company Limited. (Fig. 26).

The year of electrical recording was 1925. The process, which had been developed by H. C. Harrison and J. P. Masefield at the Bell Telephone Laboratories in the U.S.A., was adopted by Victor in America and the Gramophone Company in Britain.

Some indications that an era was coming to a close were apparent in 1929, when Edison withdrew from the entertainment side of manufacturing, although continuing to make business dictation machines in the name of Ediphone. So ended fifty-two years of pleasure-giving to millions.

Another sign of the end of the era of the 'pure' gramophone, phonograph, graphophone—whatever name the talking machine went under—was the introduction in 1929 of Britain's first Radiogram, the H.M.V. Model 520, by the Gramophone Company Limited.

The merger of the Columbia and Gramophone interests in 1931, resulting in the establishment of Electrical and Musical Industries, marks a convenient year to end this summarised history of veteran talking machines. It is also the year when the founder of the feast died—his name, Thomas Alva Edison.

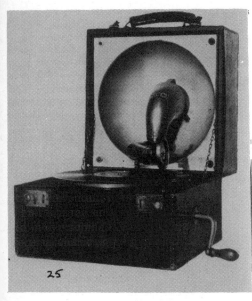

25

26

25 *Decca Portable, 1913*

26 *Gramophone Lumiere Table Model No 460*

The Truly Portable Gramophone

Before the advent of the "Decca" in 1914, to make a gramophone portable was to make it unmusical. As the size diminished, so did the sound. The volume was inadequate, the tone poor, the reproduction indistinct.

Getting right away from the ordinary principles of gramophone construction, the manufacturers of the "Decca" overcame all difficulties. They produced an instrument extraordinarily small, yet as rich and powerful in tone as the full size Cabinet gramophones—and as musical.

The "Decca" is a compact, portable gramophone which need only be visible when actually in use. At other times

"She shall have Music wherever she goes."

Taking up so little space, able to perform in any out-of-the-way corner of the room, playing in perfect time, the "Decca" is ideal for the dance.

Dancing provides another outlet for the usefulness of the "Decca." Its activities have not been confined to the home to which it belongs—"and would you mind bringing your 'Decca' with you," is a request that has often accompanied the invitation to a small dance. Taking up so little space, able to perform in any out-of-the-way corner of the room, the "Decca" has solved the musical problem for hundreds of devotees of the dance. It takes the place of the piano, for very often the piano is not in the room where the dance is to take place, or it may be that there is not a pianist available. In any case the "Decca" is more dependable, for it plays all kinds of dance music perfectly and in *faultless time*. It is like having a good orchestra in the room, with the advantage that the "Decca" never tires, whereas an orchestra has its limitations.

Always use "Decca" Needles—the best.

The possession of a good gramophone is an infinite joy both to those who like a varied musical entertainment and to lovers of more serious music. It means that whenever you feel the desire for music and whatever your mood may demand—a symphony, a song, a pianoforte or violin solo, musical comedy, humorous selections—the " Decca " is at hand to gratify your need.

* * * * *

But the pleasure of possession is one that you can share, one indeed which is enhanced by being shared with others. Your friends will appreciate the " Decca " —quite as much as you do. And on more formal occasions, when you have other visitors in your home—chance callers, with whom you are not so well acquainted—the " Decca " will help to dispel the inevitable feeling of reserve. Fetch the " Decca," put on a favourite record, and long before it has been played through the constraint will have vanished.

The pleasure of possession is one you can share. Your friends will appreciate the " Decca " Concerts —quite as much as you do.

The " Decca " is ideal for the Dance.

"They shall have music wherever they go," and here, at the seaside, they can be seen enjoying the World's greatest musicians and entertainers "all to themselves."

Of course you will take your "Decca" to the Seaside. You will have it playing on the sands; you will find it a great boon in the evenings. If you happen to have bad weather, then the "Decca" will be simply invaluable. There are few things more depressing than the seaside in wet weather; but set the "Decca" going and you will forget your determination to consult the time-table for the next train home. Maybe you are one of those who like to get away from the crowd and take their sea-side holidays in places lacking Piers and Bands and Concert Parties. Well, though you are glad to escape the noisy seaside crowds in the daytime, you often feel that what is needed to round off the day's pleasure is a good concert such as is provided at popular resorts.

Use "Decca" Needles—to get the full tone.

No need to ask if they would care to hear it. They will be as little able to mask their delight as to conceal their surprise. In a minute you will have the "Decca" playing, and long before the mysteries of the luncheon basket have been explored you will have enjoyed a concert worthy of Queen's Hall.

* * * * *

But the "Decca" is so light and compact that it may well be the constant companion of your "nearer-home" picnics, at some pretty spot within walking distance. It is one more article to carry, but it will be the life and soul of the party and make the picnic remembered for years to come.

If it is worth while taking a luncheon basket it is also worth while taking the "Decca" and a few choice records.

Music any time—anywhere.

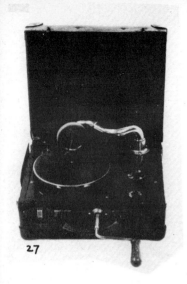

27 Acuston

28 Adler

29 Amberola I, 1909

30 Amberola IV

31 Amberola 30

32 Amberola 50

34

4. Directory of Marques, Inventors and Manufacturers

33

It cannot be claimed that the following list is a comprehensive survey of all the names connected with the complex history of talking machines. Hitherto, unknown makes are continually coming to light, and even while this book is being prepared, additions and corrections are being made. However, the directory will be useful to collectors when tracing histories of instruments.

The author is anxious to have further information about marques and manufacturers listed, as well as about those which have not been covered.

ACUSTON. A portable machine of unknown date and origin. See Specification 162. (Fig. 27).

ADLER. A camera type instrument. Probably of German origin. See Specification 163. (Fig. 28).

A.E.G., Berlin. Makers of the Magnetophon magnetic tape recorder in 1935. Also manufactured typewriters.

AJAX. A coin-operated machine made by Edison's National Phonograph Company.

ALLEGRO. A German-made machine. Known to be in production in 1912.

ALVA. An AC mains supply instrument introduced by Edison's National Phonograph Company in 1907.

AMBEROL records. Cylinders introduced by Edison's National Phonograph Company in 1908. Having twice as many grooves to the inch, they played for 4mins instead of 2mins. Blue Amberol cylinders were made from 1912.

AMBEROLA. A range of instruments introduced by Edison's National Phonograph Company in 1909 which continued to be catalogued until 1929. These were the first of the company's enclosed horn instruments. By 1913 seven models were available: I, III and IV were cabinet models; V, VI, VIII and X were table models. In 1915 the range was reduced to three: the 30, 50 and 75. See Specifications 89, 89A, 90, and 91. (Figs. 29, 30, 31, 32 and 33).

AMERICAN GRAPHOPHONE COMPANY. Formed by Bell and Tainter to make and distribute machines. In 1888 the company granted an agency to J. Lippincott of the North American Phonograph Company who leased instruments to commercial users. In 1893 production ceased and the manufacturing rights were acquired by the Columbia Phonograph Company—originally a subsidiary of the North American Phonograph Company.

AMERICAN TELEGRAPHONE COMPANY, Springfield, Mass., U.S.A. Manufacturers from 1903 of the Telegraphone magnetic recorder intended as a dictation and telephone answering apparatus.

ANGELICA. A German marque of cylinder playing instrument. Known to have been in production in 1906. (Fig. 34).

34

33 Amberola 75
34 Angelica, 1906

35

35

36.

35 Angelus, 1906

36 Parson's Auxetophone

ANGELUS. A disc playing machine made in Germany and marketed in London in 1906. (Fig. 35).

ANKER. A German made instrument. Known to have been in production in 1912.

APOLLO. A machine of Continental origin, marketed in Britain by Crais & Stavidis, London.

APOLLO No. 10. See Paillard.

AUXETOPHONE. An instrument using compressed air for amplification Developed by Horace Short who demonstrated it from the top of the Eiffel Tower in 1900. Short sold the patent rights to Charles (later Sir Charles) Parsons in 1903, who demonstrated an improved model to the Royal Society in 1904. It was built for commercial sale by Gramophone & Typewriter Limited, the cheapest model costing £100. See Specification 40. (Fig. 36).

BABY GRAND GRAMOPHONE. Introduced in 1896. This is one of the earliest instruments with a spring motor to be offered for public sale.

BABY TOURNAPHONE. See Tournaphone.

BAHRE, W; Leipzig. Started manufacturing talking machines in 1892. In 1895 Bahre collaborated with A. Koltzow to make a showman's phonograph. Bahre is believed to have been the designer of the Puck cylinder instruments.

BALMORAL. Made by Edison's National Phonograph Company. There were two models: M and E. (Fig. 39).

BARON. A Leipzig-built machine imported in 1907 by the Polyphon Supply Company, London.

BARRAUD, Francis. Artist who created the H.M.V. 'dog' or 'Nipper' trade mark. The painting was bought by W. B. Owen of the Gramophone Company Limited of London in 1899.

BEKA FLAMINGO tonearm. Used on Odeon machines, c.1912.

BEKA records. Made in Germany. By 1913 the marque was under the control of Carl Lindstrom.

BELL, Alexander Graham (1847-1922). Founder of the Volta Laboratories. With his cousin, Chichester, and Charles Tainter, produced the 'graphophone' in 1885.

BELL, Chichester. Cousin of Alexander Graham Bell. Worked on the development of the telephone and on the production of the Graphophone in 1885.

BELL records. 10½ins double-sided discs, selling at 2s 6d each. Made by Edison-Bell, London, from July 1908.

BELL TELEPHONE LABORATORIES, U.S.A. Where H. C. Harrison and J. P. Masefield developed the commercial process for electrical recording. The system was adopted by Victor, Columbia and H.M.V. from 1925.

BERLINER, Emile (1851-1929). Born in Hanover, Germany, and emigrated to Washington, DC, in 1870. In 1877 he invented and patented a microphone, the rights of which he sold to the Bell Telephone Company, and subsequently worked for Bell. Berliner devised and patented the Gramophone in 1887. By 1889 he had developed a process to make copies of discs from a zinc master. The first commercially available Gramophone was designed in 1889—a small hand-crank driven machine playing 5ins rubber discs. The instrument was manufactured by the German toy makers Kammerer & Reinhardt, and an imported version was marketed in Britain by Parkins & Gotto of Oxford Street, London. Berliner started making Gramophones in the U.S.A. in 1893; but it was not taken seriously by the public until after 1897 when Eldridge Johnson developed a spring motor for the instrument. In 1897, Berliner sent W. B. Owen to England with the commission to set up the Gramophone Company. (Figs. 37 and 38).

BERLINER GRAMOPHONE COMPANY, Philadelphia, U.S.A. Founded by Emile Berliner in 1895 to manufacture instruments and 'plates' under licence from the parent company, the United States Gramophone Company of Washington, which had been formed in 1893. See Specifications 42 and 43. (Figs. 40 and 41).

BERLINER, Joseph. Brother of Emile Berliner and manager of the company's record production at the Hanover, Germany, factory.

BERLINER TOY GRAMOPHONE. Made in 1889 by Kammerer & Reinhardt in Germany. See Specification 41. (Fig. 42).

BETTINI. American inventor who produced a cylinder machine without feed-screws in 1897. The Bettini reproducer and horn were fitted to some models of the Gramophone Type A. (Fig. 43).

BIEDERMANN & CZARNIKOW, Berlin. Established 1884. Makers of the Triumphon and Trumf instruments, and the Triumph in 1909. See Specification 164. (Fig. 44).

BIG BEN soundbox. Makers unknown. A surviving example carries the patent date as 1914.

BIJOU. A coin-operated instrument made by the National Phonograph Company.

BING PIGMYPHONE. Made in Germany by Bingwerke. Granted a British patent in 1924. See Specifications 193 and 194. (Figs. 45 and 46).

BINGOLA. Made in Germany by Bingwerke. See Specifications 195 and 196. (Figs. 47 and 48).

BLATTNERPHONE. A magnetic recorder devised by film producer, Louis Blattner, and based on the patents of Dr Kurt Stille. It was used in 1929 for adding sound to films made at Elstree Studios. The first commercial production example was purchased by the British Broadcasting Corporation in 1931.

BLUE AMBEROL records. Introduced by the National Phonograph Company in 1912. These cylinders had a plastic material surface on a plaster backing, and were intended to be played with a diamond stylus. This was one of the few marques of cylinder to survive the World War I period.

37   *Berliner Gramophone, 1888*

38   *Berliner Gramophone, c1895*

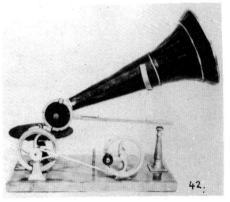

39   Edison Balmoral

40-41   Examples of Berliner Gramophones

42   Berliner Toy Gramophone

43   Columbia Graphophone A with Bettini
Reproducer and Horn

44   Trumf

45-46 *Examples of Bing Pigmyphones*

47-48 *Examples of Bingola Instruments*

49 *Brunswick 200*

50 *Brunswick 105*

51.

52

BLUE RIBBON records. 4½ins cylinders introduced by the Columbia Phonograph Company in 1908.

BRITISH OZAPHONE. Makers of the Dou-Trac Cell-o-phone magnetic tape recorder in 1937.

BRITISH ZONOPHONE COMPANY. Amalgamated with Twin Records in 1911.

BRUNSWICK-BALKE-COLLANDER COMPANY, U.S.A.

BRUNSWICK MODEL 200. Registration date in the U.S.A. 13th February 1923. Used the Ultona soundbox introduced in 1917. See Specification 92. (Fig. 49).

BRUNSWICK PANATROPE. The first electrical reproduction instrument. Made by the Brunswick company in 1925.

BRUNSWICK TABLE MODEL 105. Produced c.1921. See Specification 93. (Fig. 50).

BUSINESS PHONOGRAPH. Introduced by the National Phonograph Company in 1906.

BRUSH DEVELOPMENT COMPANY, U.S.A. Makers in 1947 of the Soundmirror, a magnetic tape recorder for home use.

BUMB & KONIG, Germany.

CAMERAPHONE. Marketed in 1924-5 by the Cameraphone Company Limited, 11 Finsbury Park, London. Models of the instrument, which was probably made in Switzerland, were priced between £3 3s and £4 10s. See Specification 165. (Fig. 51).

CHIPPENDALE. One of the seven styles of Gramophone Grand models available in 1909.

CHIPPENDALE CONSUL (CC22). The official laboratory model designed to play both 10ins and 12ins Diamond Discs. See Specification 98. (Fig. 52).

CLARION records. Marketed from 1907 at 9d each. This was one of the few marques of cylinder to survive the World War I period.

CLARK, A.W. An associate of Berliner and Johnson. Clark became chairman of the Gramophone Company.

CLARK-JOHNSON soundbox. Fitted to early Gramophones from 1897.

CLOCKWORK. An instrument introduced in 1896 by the National Phonograph Company. Later renamed the Home.

COLUMBIA 28. A badge version of the H.M.V. portable Model 102, introduced after the E.M.I. foundation.

COLUMBIA 100. Introduced in 1930. See Specification 166. (Fig. 53).

COLUMBIA 202. See Specification 167. (Fig. 54).

COLUMBIA 204. A badge version of the H.M.V. 97.

COLUMBIA BABY REGENT. A disc graphophone marketed in 1912. (Fig. 55).

COLUMBIA BIJOU. A disc graphophone marketed in 1912. (Fig. 56).

51 Cameraphone

52 Chippendale Console (CC22)

40

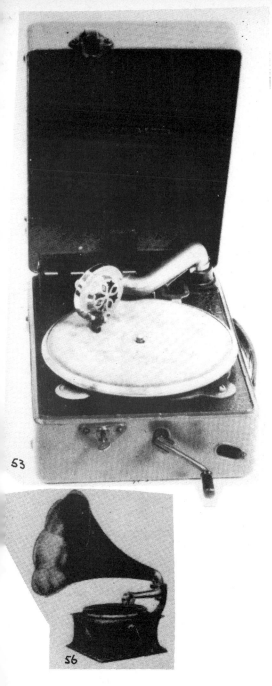

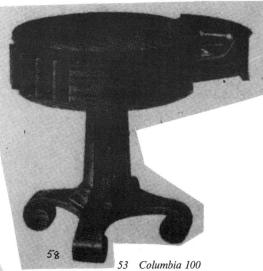

53

54

55

58

56

57

53   *Columbia 100*

54   *Columbia 202*

55   *Columbia Baby Regent*

56   *Columbia Bijou*

57   *Columbia Improved Champion*

58   *Columbia Colonial*

59.

60

COLUMBIA CHAMPION. A tonearm disc instrument marketed in the period 1905-8. (Fig. 57).

COLUMBIA COLONIAL. A disc graphophone built in the shape of a circular table marketed in 1912. (Fig. 58).

COLUMBIA CORONET. Designed to play 6ins cylinders. Introduced in 1908.

COLUMBIA CROWN. Also known as the Type BQ. Introduced in 1907, this was the first cylinder instrument to be fitted with a tonearm.

COLUMBIA DE LUXE. A disc graphophone marketed in 1912. (Fig. 59).

COLUMBIA EAGLE. Also known as the Type BX. This was the cheapest cylinder machine marketed by the Columbia Phonograph Company.

COLUMBIA ECLIPSE. A disc graphophone marketed in 1912. (Fig. 60).

COLUMBIA FAVORITE. A disc graphophone marketed in 1912. (Fig. 61).

COLUMBIA GRAFONOLA. See Grafonola.

COLUMBIA GRAPHOPHONE MODEL Q. Also known as the Mignon. Introduced in 1901.

COLUMBIA HOME PREMIER. Introduced in 1906. (Fig. 62).

COLUMBIA IMPROVED CHAMPION. A disc graphophone marketed in 1912.

COLUMBIA IMPROVED ROYAL. A disc graphophone marketed in 1912. (Fig. 63).

COLUMBIA JEWEL. Introduced in 1906 as a cheaper version of Types AZ and BK.

COLUMBIA LYRIC reproducer. Incorporated in the Type AZ of 1904.

COLUMBIA IMPERIAL. A tonearm disc instrument introduced in the 1905-8 period.

COLUMBIA MAJESTIC. A tonearm disc instrument introduced in the 1905-8 period.

COLUMBIA MIGNON. See Mignon.

COLUMBIA MIGNONETTE. A disc graphophone marketed in 1912. (Fig. 64).

COLUMBIA MULTIPLEX GRAND. A machine with three horns and sound boxes. First shown at the Paris Exposition of 1900. (Fig. 19).

COLUMBIA NONPAREIL. A disc graphophone marketed in 1912. Fig. 65).

COLUMBIA NO. 7 soundbox. Fitted to Grafonola 25A.

COLUMBIA PHONOGRAPH COMPANY, Washington, DC. Originally one of J. Lippincott's enterprises which hired both phonographs and graphophones to commercial users. Manufacture was commenced in 1888, and in 1891 the company issued what is acknowledged to be the world's first record catalogue, listing 194 titles. The American Graphophone Company was acquired in 1893, and the word 'graphophone' was given to all instruments, cylinder or disc, sold by Columbia. In 1897, the company set up its European headquarters in Paris, and a sales office in London in 1900. Towards the end of 1900, London became the European headquarters. The

59   *Columbia De Luxe*

60   *Columbia Eclipse*

61 Columbia Favorite
62 Columbia Home Premier
63 Columbia Improved Royal
64 Columbia Mignonette
65 Columbia Nonpareil
66 Columbia Princess

43

67

68.

British company bought out the American parent concern in 1923. In 1931, a merger was formed with the Gramophone Company (H.M.V.) resulting in the foundation of Electrical & Musical Industries.

COLUMBIA PRINCE. A tonearm disc instrument introduced in the 1905-8 period.

COLUMBIA PRINCESS. A disc graphophone marketed in 1912. (Fig. 66).

COLUMBIA QUADRUPLE DISC GRAPHOPHONE. First shown at the St Louis Exhibition of 1904. It had four turntables mounted on a vertical shaft, each with its own horn.

COLUMBIA REGAL. A tonearm disc machine introduced in the 1905-8 period. (Fig. 67).

COLUMBIA REGENT. A tonearm disc machine introduced in the 1905-8 period. (Fig. 68).

COLUMBIA SOVEREIGN. Introduced in 1905. Designed to play 6ins cylinders.

COLUMBIA STERLING. A tonearm disc instrument introduced in the 1905-8 period.

COLUMBIA SYMPHONY GRAND. The Columbia company's first concealed horn model, built in the shape of an upright piano. Introduced in 1907. (Fig. 69).

COLUMBIA TRUMP. Introduced in 1907 as a cheaper version of the Type AZ.

COLUMBIA TWENTIETH CENTURY PREMIER. Produced by the Columbia Phonograph Company in 1905. It was intended for use with Premier cylinders.

COLUMBIA TYPE A. See Graphophone Type A.

COLUMBIA TYPE AA. See Graphophone Type AA.

COLUMBIA TYPE AB. See Graphophone Type AB.

COLUMBIA TYPE AG. A 'grand' for large diameter records.

COLUMBIA TYPE AH. A disc machine introduced in 1903.

COLUMBIA TYPE AJ. A disc graphophone introduced in 1902. (Figs. 70 and 71).

COLUMBIA TYPE AK. A disc machine introduced in 1903.

COLUMBIA TYPE AR. A disc machine introduced in 1903.

COLUMBIA TYPE AT. A cylinder model introduced in 1898. The motor was enclosed in a wooden cabinet. See also Graphophone Type AT. (Fig. 72).

COLUMBIA TYPE AU. A disc machine introduced in 1903.

COLUMBIA TYPE AY. A disc machine introduced in 1903.

COLUMBIA TYPE AZ. A cylinder model introduced in 1904. It incorporated the Lyric reproducer. (Fig. 73).

COLUMBIA TYPE BD. A disc graphophone incorporating a tone arm. Introduced in 1906. (Fig. 74).

COLUMBIA TYPE BK. See Graphophone Type BK.

67 *Columbia Regal*

68 *Columbia Regent*

44

69   *Columbia Symphony Grand*

70   *Columbia Type AJ, 1902*

71   *Columbia Type AJ, 1903*

72   *Columbia Type AT*

73   *Columbia Type AZ*

74   *Columbia Type BD*

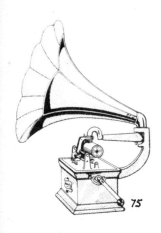

COLUMBIA TYPE BQ. Also known as the Crown. It incorporated a tonearm and was introduced in 1907. (Fig. 75).

COLUMBIA TYPE BX. Also known as the Eagle. A cheap base board machine introduced in 1898. (Fig. 76).

COLUMBIA TYPE E. See Graphophone Type E.

COLUMBIA TYPE GG. A 'grand' model for large diameter records.

COLUMBIA TYPE HAG. A 'grand' model for large diameter records.

COLUMBIA TYPE Q. Introduced in 1898 as a cheap base board model. It was extensively copied by German and Swiss manufacturers. (Fig. 77).

CONCERT. Introduced in 1899 by the National Phonograph Company as a version of the Spring Motor design. It played 5ins diameter wax cylinders. Meant to compete with the Gramophone Grand, but did not enjoy a long production period. A later model called the Concert was a renamed version of the Opera.

CONCERT AUTOMATIQUE FRANCAIS. A coin-operated machine which may or may not have been built entirely by Pathe. It was fitted with a Pathe soundbox. See Specification 44. (Fig. 78).

CONCERT soundbox. Designed by E. R. Johnson. Introduced by the Gramophone Company in 1901.

CONQUEROR. Built by the National Phonograph Company. Fitted with electric drive for either battery or mains operation.

CONSOLIDATED TALKING MACHINE COMPANY. Founded in 1899 by Eldridge R. Johnson to make the Victor Talking Machine—an instrument identical to Berliner's gramophone. In 1901, Johnson and Berliner together formed the Victor Talking Machine Company.

CRAIS & STAVIDIS, London. Marketed German-made Apollo instruments.

CROS, Charles (1842-88). Proposed a talking machine using a disc record in 1877 but did not make a model. He attempted to interest Breguet, an instrument maker, but without success. Cros practised medicine, invented a colour photography process, and was a noted poet.

CROWN. See Columbia Crown.

CRYSTALPHONE. A surviving example is marked: 'SOLE DISTRIBUTOR LARSEN DE BREY & CO. THE HAGUE. HOLLAND'. The instrument used a U.S. made Jewel soundbox. See Specification 168. (Fig. 79).

CRYSTAL records. A 4mins duration record introduced by Edison Bell in 1909 as a counter to Edison's Amberol.

CYGNET horn. An upright horn introduced by the National Phonograph Company in 1910.

DACAPO records. By 1913 this German marque was under the control of Carl Lindstrom.

DECCA. Trade mark of Barnett Samuel & Sons Limited, Worship Lane, London, E.C.

DECCA DECCALION. Available in the late 1920s. See Specification 96. Fig. 80).

75 Columbia Type BQ

76 Columbia Type BX

77.

78.

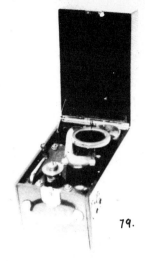

79.

80.

81

82

77   Columbia Type Q
78   Concert Automatique Francais
79   Crystalphone
80   Deccalion
81   Decca Junior Portable
82   Decca XL

83.

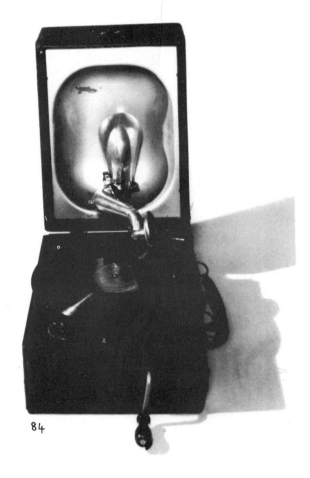

84

83-84 Examples of Decca Portables

85

86.

85-86 Examples of Decca Portables

DECCA JUNIOR PORTABLE. Made in 1925. See Specification 169. (Fig. 81).

DECCA MODEL XL. Made in 1928 with a Swiss made Telesatic soundbox. See Specification 170. (Fig. 82).

DECCA PICCADILLY. The first 'high fidelity' record player. Introduced in 1945.

DECCA PORTABLE. The first true portable machine. Manufactured by Barnett Samuel & Sons Limited from 1913. Popular with the troops in World War I. (Figs. 83, 84, 85 and 86).

DECCA SALON MODEL 130. Introduced c.1929. See Specification 171. (Fig. 87).

de FORREST, Professor Lee. Developed a magnetic recorder in 1913 for use in talking film experiments.

de HOOG & COMPANY, J., Gravenhage, The Netherlands. Assembled German-made parts and sold instruments under their own name.

DEUTSCHE EDISON GESELLSCHAFT, Cologne. Edison sold his German patent rights to this company.

DEUTSCHE GRAMMOPHON AKTIENGESELLSCHAFT. A subsidiary of the Gramophone Company in London. Makers of the Zonophone instruments and records for the cheaper market as well as products under the parent company label. One machine was made in the shape of a piano. See Specification 97. (Fig. 88).

DEUXPHONE. Introduced in 1905. Designed to play both cylinders and discs. Not a success.

D.G.A. See Deutsche Grammophon Aktiengesellschaft.

DIAMOND DISC PHONOGRAPH. See Edison Diamond Disc.

DIAMOND MODEL B reproducer. Used on Home Model A (1901-5) and Triumph Model A instruments.

DICTAPHONE. Introduced in 1908 by the Columbia Phonograph Company for use with Premier cylinders.

DISCAPHONE. Made by Edison Bell from 1908 to play both needle-cut and phono-cut discs. (Fig. 89).

DISC GRAPHOPHONE. Produced by the American Graphophone Company from 1903. The Type AJ was the first instrument to carry this name.

DON. Made in England by Edison Bell from 1907.

DOUBLE EAGLE. See Graphophone Type AB.

DOU-TRAC CELL-O-PHONE. A magnetic tape recorder made by the British Ozaphone company in 1937.

DRAWING ROOM PHONOGRAPH. Supplied on hire at £10 p.a. by the Edison Bell Phonograph Corporation Limited, London, from 1892.

DULCEPHONE. Marketed by Barnett Samuel.

DULCETTO. Maker not known. The instrument is a copy of the Columbia Type BX (The Eagle).

87 Decca Salon 130

88 Deutsche Grammophon Gramola in Piano Case

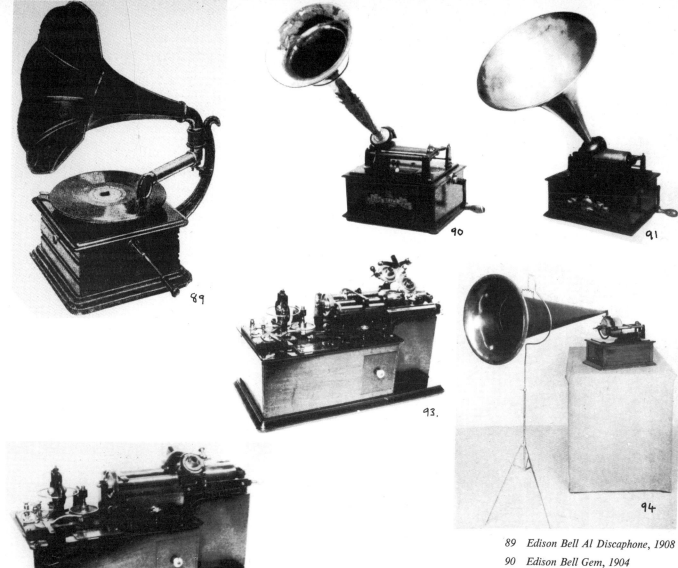

89   *Edison Bell Al Discaphone, 1908*
90   *Edison Bell Gem, 1904*
91   *Edison Bell Gem*
92   *Edison Class M*
93   *Edison Class S*
94   *Edison Concert, 1899*

95.

96

DURINOID COMPANY, Newark, New Jersey. Makers of the material Durinoid which was used in the manufacture of buttons. In 1897, the Gramophone Company started to use Durinoid for the production of records.

E.B. (Edison Bell) records. Needle-cut records made by J. E. Hough and priced at 2s 6d each.

EAGLE. See Columbia Eagle.

EBONY records. Made from 1898 by Edisonia Limited.

EDIPHONE. Trade name given to business dictation cylinder machines which continued in production after Edison gave up the entertainment side of manufacture in 1929.

EDISON AMBEROLA. Model 1 was introduced in 1909.

EDISON BELL CONSOLIDATED PHONOGRAPH COMPANY, London, Formed in 1898 as a result of a merger between Edisonia Limited and the Edison Bell Phonograph Corporation Limited, with J. E. Hough as managing director. A factory in Peckham, south east London, was opened in 1903.

EDISON BELL PHONOGRAPH CORPORATION LIMITED. The British patent rights of both Edison, and Bell and Tainter were sold to this company in 1892. Phonographs were hired to commercial concerns as dictation machines at £10 p.a. Drawing Room Phonographs were hired at the same fee, but these did not have recording facilities. Altogether, some 700 machines were hired. In 1898 the company was merged with Edisonia Limited and the Edison Bell Consolidated Phonograph Company was formed.

EDISON BELL GEM. Made in England from 1904. See Specification 9. (Figs. 90 and 91).

EDISON CLASS M PHONOGRAPH. Surviving examples show 1888 as the latest patent date. See Specification 10. (Fig. 92).

EDISON CLASS S PHONOGRAPH. Made from 1893 and imported by the Edison Bell Phonograph Corporation Limited, London. See Specification 11. (Fig. 93).

EDISON CONCERT. Produced between 1899 and 1901. See Specification 12. (Figs. 94 and 95).

EDISON cylinders. In 1906 the length of these cylinders was slightly increased and prices reduced from 1s 6d to 1s.

EDISON DIAMOND DISC PHONOGRAPH. MODEL C200. Introduced by the National Phonograph Company in 1912-13. In 1927 a version was produced that could play a 12ins disc for 20mins a side at 80rpm. See Specification 99. (Fig. 96).

EDISON DUPLEX REPRODUCER. Introduced in 1896 for the use of showmen. It used two trumpet horns facing in opposite directions. (Fig. 97).

EDISONIA LIMITED, London. Established by J. E. Hough in 1897 to sell imported machines and records. In 1898 the company was reorganised as the Edison Bell Consolidated Phonograph Company and merged with Edison Bell Phonograph Corporation Limited. Edisonia Limited continued as a

95   Edison Concert

96   Edison Diamond Disc Phonograph C200

97   *Edison Duplex Reproducer, 1896*
98   *Edison Phonograph, 1888*
99   *Edison Bell Elf, 1907*
100 *l'Enchantresse, 1906*

101

102

manufacturing unit, producing Popular, Ebony, Indestructible and Grand Concert records. A factory was acquired in Peckham, south east London in 1903, to produce Gold Moulded records and phonographs. Edisonia bought out the Edison Bell company outright in 1908 and the name was changed to J. E. Hough Limited.

EDISON OPERA. See Opera.

EDISON PHONOGRAPH WORKS. Founded by Thomas Alva Edison to manufacture phonographs. A sales agency was granted to J. Lippincott of the North American Phonograph Company in 1888.

EDISON PARLOUR SPEAKING PHONOGRAPH. Marketed in 1878 by the Edison Speaking Phonograph Company. The selling price was $10.

EDISON SPEAKING PHONOGRAPH COMPANY, 200 Broadway, New York. Formed by Thomas Alva Edison in April 1878, with the main role of hiring instruments to travelling showmen who paid a percentage of their receipts to the company.

EDISON, Thomas Alva (1847-1931), West Orange, New Jersey. As a result of work on telephone repeater mechanisms, he constructed his first voice reproducing instrument in 1877. Further experiments were made, and in June 1888 the invention was ready for commercial exploitation. The National Phonograph Company was formed in 1895. Edison abandoned the entertainment side of the talking machine market in 1929. (Fig. 98).

EDMUNDS, Henry. After seeing an Edison demonstration in the U.S.A., Edmunds wrote newspaper articles on the subject of phonographs. These aroused the interest of William Preece, Chief Engineer to the G.P.O., who asked Edmunds and an engineering colleague, A. Stroh, to build a tinfoil phonograph which Preece demonstrated before the Royal Institution in February 1878.

ELECTRICAL AND MUSICAL INDUSTRIES. Formed in 1931 as the result of a merger between the Gramophone and Columbia companies in London.

ELF. An instrument made by Edison Bell from 1907. Modifications were made in 1909 to enable Crystal records to be played. (Fig. 99).

E.M.I. See Electrical and Musical Industries.

l'ENCHANTRESSE. A German make of cylinder machine marketed in London in 1906. (Fig. 100).

ERA. Made in England by Edison Bell from 1907.

EXCELDA. An instrument fitted with a Swiss-made motor. See Specification 172. (Fig. 101).

EXCELLENCE. A portable machine. Origin and production dates not known. See Specification 173. (Fig. 102).

EXCELLENT NO. 51. Appeared in the 1912-13 catalogue of Carl Schroeder of Berlin.

EXCELSIOR. Made by a German company founded in 1899 which produced instruments closely resembling the Columbia models. The factory was situated at Nippes, Cologne, and production lasted at least up to 1912. The chief selling outlets were through W. Bahre and the Holzweissig Company of Leipzig. They were imported and marketed in London in 1906. See Specification 28. (Figs. 103 and 104).

EXHIBITION soundbox. Developed by Jones and Gibson. It was marketed from 1902-3 and fitted to almost all Gramophone Company instruments made between 1905 and 1919. Up to the outbreak of World War I, it was imported into England from the Victor company in the U.S.A. All Hayes, England, manufactured Exhibition soundboxes are marked 'His Master's Voice'.

EXPOSITION soundbox. Fitted to a German-made camera style instrument.

FAVORITA. A German make of cylinder playing instrument marketed in London in 1906. (Fig. 105).

FAVORITE. Made in Germany. By 1913 the production was under the control of Carl Lindstrom.

FERRIS, E.A. Holder of the British patent covering the Peter Pan instrument in the form of a camera. Made in Switzerland.

FEUCHT und FABI, Germany. Makers of talking machine accessories.

FIRESIDE. Models A and B. Introduced by Edison's National Company in 1909. Now rare. See Specification 13. (Figs. 106, 107 and 108).

FLORAPHONE. Made in Germany c.1907.

FONOTIPIA. Made in Germany. By 1913 the production was under the control of Carl Lindstrom.

FORTOPHON STARKTONMASCHINE. A public hall instrument using compressed air for amplification. (Fig. 109).

GAISBERG, Fred W. An American who came to England to manage the recording policy of the Gramophone Company, recording some of the greatest names in the operatic field. Gaisberg played the piano for the first disc to be produced by the Gramophone Company in 1898.

GAUMONT ELGEPHONE. A French-made public hall instrument, using a gas flame in a method of amplification.

GAYDON, H. A. Inventor and constructor of the Stentorphone of 1910.

GEM. Models A, B, C, D, and E. Introduced in 1899 by the National Phonograph Company, and made in England from 1904 by Edison Bell. The Model D was known as the Red Gem. See Specifications 14, 15 and 16. (Figs. 110, 111 and 112).

GETRAPHON. A German-made instrument using a Swiss Maestrophone Maestro soundbox. (Fig. 113).

GILBERT. Made by Gilbert & Company, Sheffield, and carried the slogan 'The World's Best Music'. Sold in the late 1920s. See Specification 104. (Fig. 114).

GINN, E. M., London. Maker of hand-built talking machines. (Fig. 115).

GOLDKLONG NO. 25 soundbox. Fitted to some instruments made in 1914.

103

104.

103 Excelsior, 1906

104 Excelsior

55

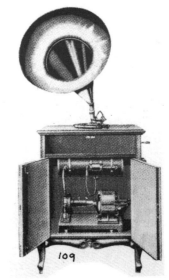

105 *Favorita, 1906*

106 *Edison Fireside Model A*

107-108 *Edison Fireside Model B*

109 *Fortophone Starkrenmaschine*

110 *Edison Gem Model A*

111 *Edison Gem Model B/C*

112 *Edison Gem Model D/E*

113 *Getraphon*

114 *Gilbert*

115 *E. M. Ginn Handmade Gramophone*

57

116.

117

116 *Columbia Grafonola 22A*

117 *Columbia Grafonola 25A*

GOLD MOULDED records. Made from 1903 by the Edison Bell Consolidated Phonograph Company at their Peckham factory.

GRAFONOLA 22A. Made in Britain by Columbia. Similar in design to 25A. See Specification 94. (Fig. 116).

GRAFONOLA 25A. Made in Britain by Columbia. Fitted with Garrard electric motor. Produced from the mid-1920s. See Specification 95. (Fig. 117).

GRAMOPHONE. This was the name given to the invention of Emile Berliner in 1887. It was used on products of the Gramophone Company until the sole rights were lost in a court action of 1909.

GRAMOPHONE CABINET GRAND NO. 180. Produced from 1923 for one year only. Originally fitted with a No. 2 soundbox and then with No. 4. See Specification 105. (Fig. 118).

GRAMOPHONE COMPANY, 31 Maiden Lane, Strand, London. Established in 1898 by W. B. Owen, who was sent to England by Berliner to form a marketing organisation for Europe. In that year a factory was set up in Hanover to produce records for the European market. A studio was included at Maiden Lane in addition to a workshop for assembling instruments. In 1900 the name was changed to Gramophone & Typewriter Limited but it reverted to the Gramophone Company Limited in November 1907.

Owen bought Francis Barraud's painting, 'His Master's Voice', in 1899 but it did not become the company's official trade mark until 1910—the 'Recording Angel' being the main trade mark up till then.

A new factory was built at Hayes, Middlesex, in 1907. Records were pressed there which had hitherto been produced in Hanover, where the manager was Joseph Berliner.

The Gramophone Company Limited was merged with the Columbia Company in 1931 to form the Electrical and Musical Industries. (Figs. 119 and 120).

GRAMOPHONE CZ. See Gramophone Model 12.

GRAMOPHONE GRAND. Known in the U.S.A. as the Victor Victoria. This was the first internal-horn instrument to be introduced by Gramophone & Typewriter Limited in 1907. The horn was made from cast iron and plywood. By 1909, seven styles, including Chippendale, Sheraton and Queen Anne, were available. (Fig. 121).

GRAMOPHONE HORNLESS MODEL 1. Introduced in 1910 to replace the Pigmy Grand. In production until 1924. See Specification 106. (Figs. 122 and 123).

GRAMOPHONE HORNLESS MODEL 3. Made between 1913 and 1917. Fitted with the Exhibition soundbox. See Specification 107. (Fig. 124).

GRAMOPHONE HORNLESS MODEL NO. 60. Produced from 1920 until 1924—all hornless models were dropped in that year. First sold with the Exhibition soundbox, then with No. 2. See Specification 108. (Fig. 125).

118 *Gramophone Cabinet Grand No 180*
119 *Gramophone 'Dog Model', 1898*
120 *Gramophone, c1902*
121 *Gramophone Grand, 1907*
122 *Gramophone Hornless No 1*
123 *Gramophone Hornless No 1 (L.B.A.O.)*

124 *Gramophone Hornless No 3*

125 *Gramophone Hornless No 60*

126 *Gramophone Library Bijou Grand*

127 *Gramophone Lumiere Combined Gramophone and Wireless*

128 *Gramophone Model VII*

129 *Gramophone Model VIIA*

60

GRAMOPHONE LIBRARY BIJOU GRAND. Produced in 1909. Later redesignated No. 10. See Specification 110. (Fig. 126).

GRAMOPHONE LUMIERE COMBINED GRAMOPHONE AND WIRELESS. The model incorporated a 2-valve crystal set. See Specification 51. (Fig. 127).

GRAMOPHONE MODEL 7. Introduced in late 1910. From 1912 it was known as the Model 7A. Originally fitted with the Exhibition soundbox and later with the No. 4. The model was in production until 1913. See Specifications 58 & 59. (Figs. 128 and 129).

GRAMOPHONE MODEL 8. The first of the Gramophone Company's table grand introduced in 1910. (Fig. 130).

130

GRAMOPHONE MODEL 12. When exported, the model was known as the CZ. In production between 1910 and 1912. Fitted with the Exhibition soundbox. See Specification 111. (Fig. 131).

GRAMOPHONE MODEL 109. Introduced in 1925. Fitted with the No. 4 soundbox. See Specification 112. (Fig. 132).

GRAMOPHONE MODEL 125. Produced 1922 and 1924. Fitted with the No. 2 soundbox. See Specification 113. (Fig. 133).

GRAMOPHONE MODEL 130. Produced between 1929 and 1931. Fitted with the No. 5A soundbox. See Specification 114. (Fig. 134).

GRAMOPHONE MODEL 157. The smallest of the re-entrant models. Fitted with the No. 5A soundbox. See Specification 115. (Fig. 135).

GRAMOPHONE MODEL 163. A re-entrant model introduced in 1927. Fitted with the No. 5A soundbox. See Specification 116. (Fig. 136).

131.

GRAMOPHONE MODEL 265. Produced between 1922 and 1924. Fitted with the No. 2 soundbox. See Specification 117. (Fig 137).

GRAMOPHONE MODEL 461. Available from 1926 until 1928. The case was designed for Lumiere models. Fitted with the No. 4 soundbox. See Specification 118. (Fig. 138).

GRAMOPHONE STYLE DE LUXE. Introduced in 1900 by the Gramophone & Typewriter Company.

GRAMOPHONE STYLE NO. 2. A hand-driven instrument introduced by the Gramophone Company in 1898, priced at £2 2s. Fitted with the Clark-Johnson soundbox. See Specification 53. (Figs. 139 and 140).

GRAMOPHONE STYLE NO. 3. Originally designated Style No. 5. Renumbered in 1904 after modifications which included a brake and larger spring. Introduced in 1900.

GRAMOPHONE STYLE NO. 4. Introduced by the Gramophone Company in 1900.

GRAMOPHONE STYLE NO. 5. Introduced in 1898 when it was priced at £5 10s. Known as the 'dog' model as it carried 'His Master's Voice' picture. Renamed Style No. 3 in 1904. The model was later evolved into the Junior Monarch range. (Fig. 141).

130 Gramophone No 8, 1910
131 Gramophone Model 12 (CZ)

132 Gramophone No 109
133 Gramophone No 125
134 Gramophone No 130
135 Gramophone Upright Grand No 157
136 Gramophone Upright Grand No 163
137 Gramophone No 265

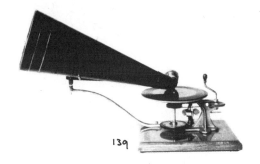

139

140.

138

141

142

143.

138 Gramophone No 461

139 Gramophone Style No 2

140 Gramophone Style No 2

141 Gramophone Style No 5, 1900

142 Gramophone Upright Grand No 202

143 Columbia Graphophone

144

145

GRAMOPHONE STYLE NO. 6. Introduced by the Gramophone Company in 1900.

GRAMOPHONE STYLE NO. 7. Made by Gramophone & Typewriter Limited from 1900.

GRAMOPHONE & TYPEWRITER LIMITED. The title given to the Gramophone Company in 1900. Apart from the gramophone, the company also marketed the Lambert typewriter, sales of which were discontinued in 1904. The word 'Typewriter' was dropped from the company's style in November 1907. See Specification 46.

GRAMOPHONE TYPE II. See Intermediate Monarch.

GRAMOPHONE UPRIGHT GRAND NO. 202. Introduced in 1927 with the No. 5A soundbox. The model used the 'matched impedance' system developed by Westinghouse Electric. See Specification 121. (Fig. 142).

GRAND CONCERT records. Made from 1898 by Edisonia Limited.

GRAMOPHONE NO. 2 soundbox. Introduced 1921.

GRAMOPHONE NO. 4 soundbox. Introduced 1924.

GRAMOPHONE NO. 5 and NO. 5A soundboxes. Introduced 1927.

GRAPHOPHONE. Produced by Alexander Graham Bell, Chichester Bell and Charles Tainter at the Volta Laboratories in 1894. The name 'Graphophone' was given to all instruments, disc or cylinder, made by the Columbia company. (Fig. 143).

GRAPHOPHONE TYPE A. Produced from 1898, in the U.S.A. Some models were fitted with the Bettini reproducer and horn. See Specifications 1 and 2. (Fig. 144).

GRAPHOPHONE TYPE AA. Produced between c.1900 and 1901 in the U.S.A. It was more ornate than earlier models. See Specification 3. (Fig. 145).

GRAPHOPHONE TYPE AB. Production period c.1900-1901 in the U.S.A. Designed to play 5ins wax cylinders. The model was also known as the Double Eagle. See Specification 4. (Fig. 146).

GRAPHOPHONE TYPE AJ. U.S.-made and introduced in 1902. It was known as the 'Disc Graphophone'.

GRAPHOPHONE TYPE AT. Produced in the U.S.A. between 1898 and 1904. See Specification 5. (Fig. 147).

GRAPHOPHONE TYPE BK. Made in the U.S.A. Fitted with the Improved Lyric reproducer. The model was also known as the 'Jewel'. See Specification 6. (Fig. 148).

GRAPHOPHONE TYPE BX. Introduced in the U.S.A. in 1898 and withdrawn in 1901. The model was also known as 'The Eagle'. See Specification 7. (Figs. 149 and 150).

GRAPHOPHONE TYPE E. Made in the U.S.A. and powered by a 2 volt wet-cell battery. See Specification 8. (Fig. 151).

GRAPHOPHONE TYPE Q. Introduced in the U.S.A. in 1898.

144 *Columbia Graphophone A*

145 *Columbia Graphophone AA*

149.

147

150.

146

148

151.

146 Columbia Graphophone AB
147 Columbia Graphophone AT
148 Columbia Graphophone BK
149 Columbia Graphophone BX Eagle
150 Columbia Graphophone BX Eagle
151 Columbia Graphophone Type E

65

152.

153.

GREENHILL, J. E. A London schoolmaster who, in 1883, built a phonograph with a spring motor, thought to have been the first with such a drive.

GRUBU 4 motor. Made in Germany.

HAIN, Stephan. Krefeld, Germany. Maker of Klingsor instruments.

HARDY TINFOIL PHONOGRAPH. Produced in 1878 by E. Hardy of Le Phonographe Edison, Paris. See Specification 29. (Fig. 152).

HIGH SPEED (TYPE XP) records. Discs made by the Columbia Phonograph Company in 1900, at the time when the European headquarters were moved to London.

HILLER, B. Berlin. Manufactured a speaking clock in 1911. The prototype machine used a perforated celluloid strip, later models used a disc.

HIS MASTER'S VOICE. A picture painted by Francis Barraud. This was purchased by W. B. Owen of the Gramophone Company in 1899 and later used as the company's trade mark.

H.M.V. NO. 2 soundbox. Cabinet models of the Gramophone Company were fitted with No. 2 soundboxes from 1921. Used in conjunction with a tapered gooseneck tonearm.

H.M.V. NO. 4 soundbox. Introduced in 1924 to meet the needs of electrical recording. It incorporated a larger diaphram and thin swan-neck tonearm.

H.M.V. NO. 5A soundbox. Replacement of the No. 16 soundbox.

H.M.V. NO. 5B soundbox. Fitted from 1927.

H.M.V. NO. 16 soundbox. A cheap non-replaceable soundbox, similar in appearance to the No. 5A. The No. 16 was fitted to the Model 102 portable.

H.M.V. AUTOMATIC GRAMOPHONE. Introduced 1927-8. It had a 43ins high cabinet and was fitted with a No. 5A soundbox, electric motor and automatic record-changer. Remote control was provided from a free-standing ash-tray type pedestal. A maximum of 20 records could be stacked. Priced at £125. In 1930 a No. 12 Automatic Gramophone was introduced, priced between £75 and £80, according to cabinet. See Specification 122. (Fig. 153).

H.M.V. ELECTRICAL REPRODUCER NO. 551. Introduced in 1929. See Specification 123. (Fig. 154).

H.M.V. MODEL 97. A badge version of the design shared by the Columbia 204. It was fitted with the pre-merger (1931) Columbia soundbox.

H.M.V. MODEL 101. See H.M.V. Portable.

H.M.V. MODEL 102. See H.M.V. Portable.

H.M.V. MODELS 202 and 203. Pre-entrant tone-chamber instruments with the horn divided into four sections and re-united at the mouth. Introduced 1927-8.

H.M.V. MODEL 520 RADIO-GRAMOPHONE. Introduced in 1929 as the first British made radiogram. A table model, the H.M.V. 501, was marketed in 1931.

H.M.V. MODEL 600 CONCERT GRAMOPHONE. Introduced in 1927. This model was the first electrical reproducing gramophone to be built in England.

152 Hardy Tinfoil Phonograph

153 H.M.V. Automatic Gramophone No 12

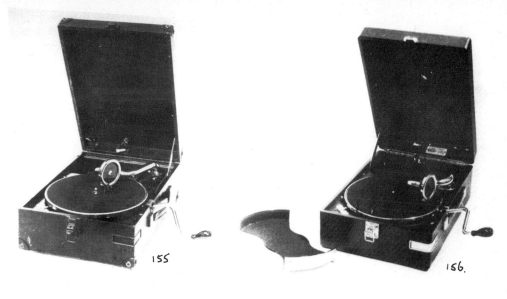

154

155

156.

157

158

159

154 *Gramophone Electrical Reproducer No 551*
155 *H.M.V. 101*
156 *H.M.V. 102*
157 *Edison Home Model A/B*
158 *Edison Home Model C/D*
159 *Edison Home Model E/F/G*

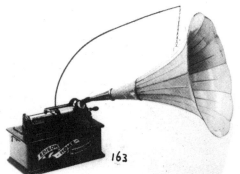

160 *Edison Home Model A*
161 *Edison Home Model A*
162 *Edison Home Model A*
163 *Edison Home Model B*
164 *Edison Home Model B*

H.M.V. PORTABLE. MODEL 101 introduced in 1928, *MODEL 102* in 1929. Heavier machines than their Decca counterparts. After the Columbia/ Gramophone merger in 1931, there were several badge variations of the portable, including a Columbia model of the 102 fitted with a No. 5B soundbox. Instruments based on the Model 102 were sold until the 1950s. See Specifications 174 and 175. (Figs. 155 and 156).

H.M.V. TABLE GRAND NO. 109. Introduced in 1925, fitted with a No. 4 soundbox. See Specification 124.

HOLZWEISSIG, Leipzig. Maker of Goliath and Hymnophon, as well as factoring Excelsior.

HOME. Models A, B, C, D, E, F, and G. Originally known as the Clockwork, when it was introduced in 1896 (some sources give this date as 1898) by the National Phonograph Company. The instrument had provision for home recording. Model B was introduced in 1906. See Specifications 17, 18, 19, 20. (Figs. 157, 158, 159, 160, 161, 162, 163 and 164).

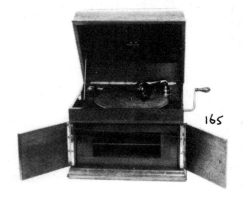
165

HOMOCORD ELECTRO. A German made instrument of the mid-1920s. (Figs. 165 and 166).

HOMOPHONE records. Made in Germany. By 1913 the marque was under the control of Carl Lindstrom.

HORIZONTAL GRAND. See Gramophone Model 265.

HOUGH, J. E. (1848-1925). Imported phonographs for use by showmen. Set up the London Phonograph Company, and Edisonia Limited in 1897. Although sued by Edison Bell, he continued his importing and selling activities and, in 1898, merged with the Edison Bell Phonograph Company to form the Edison Bell Consolidated Phonograph Company. Hough purchased the company outright in 1908 and the name was changed to J. E. Hough Limited.

HUMANN, Clemens. Germany. Maker, from 1910, of the Riesen-Lyra horn.

HYMNOPHON. A German marque introduced in 1903-4 by Holzweissig of Leipzig. Instruments were made in shapes as varied as beer barrels and grottoes. See Specifications 125 and 176. (Figs. 167, 168 and 169).

IDEAL. A model introduced by National Phonograph Company in 1917.

IDELIA. Models D1 and D2. Made by the National Phonograph Company. (Figs. 170 and 171).

IMP. Made in England by Edison Bell from 1907.

IMPROVED LYRIC reproducer. Fitted to some Columbia models.

INDESTRUCTIBLE records. Made from 1898 by Edisonia Limited.

INDESTRUCTIBLE RECORD COMPANY, Albany, New York. Sales were taken over in 1909 by the Columbia Phonograph Company. In that year a 4min cylinder was introduced, which was imported into England by Murdoch. One of the few makes of cylinder to survive the World War I period.

INDUPHON 138. An instrument fitted with a motor by Original Steidinger-motore, St Georgen, Black Forest. See Specification 197. (Fig. 172).

166.

165-166 Homocord Electro

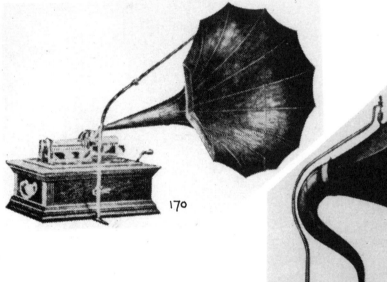

167 Hymophon, 1909

168 Hymnophon

169 Hymnophon

170 Edison Idelia Model D1

171 Edison Idelia Model D2

172 Induphon

70

INDUSTIA METALWERK FABRIK. Makers of metal horns.

INTERMEDIATE MONARCH. Introduced by the Gramophone Company in 1908 (some sources give the date as 1910). Fitted with an Exhibition soundbox, and selling for £4 10s. The model was also known as the Gramophone Type II. See Specification 60. (Fig. 173).

INTERNATIONAL TALKING MACHINE COMPANY, Weissensee, near Berlin, Makers of Odeon records. The first double-sided Odeon appeared in 1904.

INTERNATIONAL ZONOPHONE COMPANY. The European headquarters were established in Berlin in 1901. A London office was set up but the interests were purchased by Gramophone & Typewriter Limited in 1903, the name—Zonophone—surviving as a badge marque on some Gramophone Company products.

IRVINE, Archibald H. Builder of a modified tinfoil phonograph in 1878 for W. H. Preece's lectures. (Fig. 174).

JEWEL. See Gramophone Types BK and AZ.

JEWEL PHONOPARTS COMPANY, Chicago.

JEWEL soundbox. Made in the U.S.A. Fitted to the Crystalphone.

JOHNSON, Eldridge R. (1866-1945). Developed and manufactured a spring motor drive for Berliner's gramophone in 1897. Founder of the Consolidated Talking Machine Company in 1899 which built the Gramophone under the name Victor Talking Machine. Berliner joined Johnson in 1901 and the Victor Talking Machine Company was formed, with Johnson in control.

JONES, J. Worked in Berliner's factory. Patentee of a process of stamping discs using a shellac-based material. The patent application was made in 1897 and granted four years later. Manufacturing rights were purchased by the American Graphophone Company.

JUMBO records. Made in Germany. By 1913 the marque was under the control of Carl Lindstrom.

JUNIOR GRAND. Made by the Gramophone Company in 1909. British-made cabinets were in mahogany and German productions were in oak. The tonearm was similar to that of the Pigmy Grand. Price in Britain: £12 10s. See Specification 109. (Fig. 175).

JUNIOR MONARCH. Introduced by Gramophone & Typewriter Limited in October 1902, priced at £5 10s and fitted with the Concert soundbox. Designed to play 10ins records. The main variations of the Junior Monarch were: 1902—with top wind. 1903—with side wind. 1904 (early)—with tonearm. 1904 (late)—with tapered tonearm. 1905—with a 'flower' horn. The case was redesigned in 1908. See Specifications 48, 49, 57. (Figs. 176, 177, 178, 179, 180, 181, 182 and 183).

KALLIOPE. Made in Germany. Known to have been in production in 1912.

KAMERAPHONE. (Fig. 184).

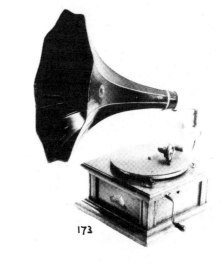

173

174.

173 Gramophone Type II Intermediate Monarch

174 Irvine's Modified Tinfoil Phonograph

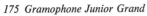

175

176

177

178

179

180

175 *Gramophone Junior Grand*

176 *Gramophone Junior Monarch, 1902*

177 *Gramophone Junior Monarch, 1903*

178 *Gramophone Junior Monarch, early 1904*

179 *Gramophone Junior Monarch, late 1904*

180 *Gramophone Junior Monarch, 1905*

181

182.

183

184.

185.

186

181-183 Gramophone Junior Monarch
184 Kameraphone

73

187

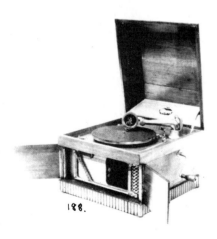

188.

185 Klingsor, 1908

186 Klingsor Verdi

KAMMERER & REINHARDT, Waltershaven, Germany. Toy manufacturers who made Berliner's Gramophone from 1889.

KASTENPUCK. Also known as the Lohengrin. A cabinet based Puck cylinder instrument made from 1905.

KLINGSOR. A German instrument introduced in 1908 by Stephan Hain of Krefeld, and Polyphon Musikwerke, Leipzig. For some obscure reason, strings were stretched across the mouth of the horn. There was a Klingsor Verdi machine which was introduced into Britain in 1912, and coin-operated instruments appeared with the Klingsor badge. Marketed in England by Murdoch until 1914. See Specifications 126, 127, 128, 129. (Figs. 185, 186, 187, 188 and 189).

KOLTZOW, A. Founder of the phonograph industry in Cologne from 1890. In 1895 Koltzow collaborated with W. Bahre to produce a showman's phonograph.

KONIG. Maker of scientific and acoustic instruments, including Scott de Martinville's phonautograph from 1859.

KRUESI, John. Thomas Edison's mechanic who actually constructed the 1877 machine.

LARSEN DE BREY & COMPANY, The Hague, Netherlands. Distributor of the Crystalphone.

LEMIPHONE. Instrument carrying an 'LM' trademark. See Specification 198. (Fig. 190).

LINDSTROM, Carl. Berlin. Started talking machine manufacture in 1896. One of the makers who produced Puck cylinder instruments. By 1913 Lindstrom controlled sales of Beka, Decapo, Favorite, Fonotipia, Homophon, Lyraphon, Jumbo and Odeon records, as well as Lindstrom's own marque of Parlaphone. Lindstrom was probably the maker of the 1912 Mignon.

LIORET, Henri J. France. Inventor of a cylinder machine without feed-screws in 1896—a model was demonstrated to the Societe Francaise de Physique in 1897. Instruments and records were given the trade name Lioretgraph. A Lioret Model C instrument was introduced in 1900. Also in that year, Lioret produced an instrument called Le Merveilleux, which was imported by Rowe & Company, 15 Aldermanbury Street, London—the sole agents in Britain. Lioret at one time worked in association with Pathe Freres. See Specifications 30 and 177. (Figs. 191, 192 and 193).

LIORET DOLL 'BEBE JUMEAU'. A phonograph for building into dolls was patented in Britain in 1893. The first production example was made for Tzar Nicholas's daughter in 1895. The doll was still catalogued in 1900.

LIORETGRAPH. The trade name used by Henri J. Lioret. An instrument carrying this name was exhibited at the Bordeaux Exposition of 1895. Model Nos. 2 and 3 were introduced in 1900. See Specification 178. (Figs. 194 and 195).

LIPPINCOTT, J. Founder of the North American Phonograph Company to exploit the talking machine. Between 1888 and 1893 he was in control of

189.

190

191

192

193

194.

187-188 *Klinsor Verdi*
189 *Klingsor Verdi*
190 *Lemiphone*
191-192 *Lioret Model C*
193 *Lioret Le Merveilleux*
194 *Lioretograph No 3, 1900*

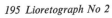

195 *Lioretograph No 2*

196 *Puck Lohengrin (Kastenpuck), 1905*

197 *London Console (LC 38)*

198 *London No 1 (L 35)*

199 *London (L 35)*

200 *London Stereoscopic Company Tinfoil*
Phonograph

several companies which were hiring Edison's phonographs and Bell and Tainter's graphophones. One of these enterprises was the Columbia Phonograph Company which, in 1894, marketed an improved spring-driven Graphophone.

LITTLE CHAMPION records. Phono-cut discs made by J. E. Hough Limited, London.

LOCHMANN, Paul. German maker of the polyphon from c.1885, in collaboration with Elias Parr in England.

LOCKWOOD, London. Marketed the Perophone instrument.

LOHENGRIN. Also known as the Kastenpuck. Built from 1905, it was a cabinet-based Puck cylinder instrument. (Fig. 196).

LONDON CONSOLE (*LC 38*). Designed to play Edison Diamond Discs. See Specification 101. (Fig. 197).

LONDON NO. 1 (*LC 35*). Like the London Console (LC 38), this instrument was designed to play Edison Diamond Discs. See Specifications 100, 102. (Figs. 198 and 199).

LONDON PHONOGRAPH COMPANY. Founded by J. E. Hough, who imported instruments for use by showmen. Hough produced records as early as c.1892.

LONDON POPULAR CYLINDERS. Introduced in the 1905-7 period.

LONDON STEREOSCOPIC COMPANY, Cheapside and Regent Street, London. Licensed by Edison to build phonographs in Britain towards the end of 1878 to sell at £10 10s. The indenture lasted until 1891. The 1896 catalogue listed three versions:
1. Hand-cranked instrument without flywheel, £5.
2. With flywheel, £10 10s.
3. Drive by falling weight, £25.
(Fig. 200).

LONGEST PLAYING PHONE. A project of the National Gramophone Company in 1908, using 16ins cylinders. It was abandoned at an early stage. (Fig. 201).

LORELEI. A Puck cylinder machine, made from 1906. (Fig. 202).

LUMIERE, Louis. Inventor in 1909 of the pleated diaphragm and granted British Patent No. 11015. Several Lumiere models were marketed by the Gramophone Company from October 1924 until 1927. The device was made from varnished paper, taking the place of the conventional soundbox, tone-arm and horn. The Gramophone Lumiere Model No. 460 was a table instrument and No. 510 a cabinet grand. See Specifications 50, 51, 52. (Fig. 203).

LYRA. A Puck machine with a 'flower' horn, made from 1905.

LYRAPHONE records. Made in Germany. By 1913, the marque was under the control of Carl Lindstrom.

LYRIC. See Columbia Eagle.

MAE STARR TALKING DOLL. Made in the U.S.A. in the 1930s.

201 Longest Playing Phone, 1908

202 Puck Lorelei, 1906

77

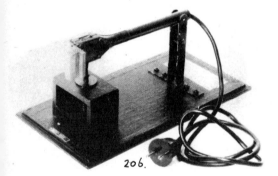

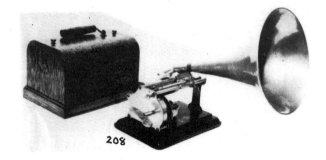

203 *Gramophone Lumiere Cabinet Grand No 510*

204 *Magnet, 1906*

205 *Melophone*

206 *Micoton*

207 *Mignon*

208 *Columbia Graphophone Q (Mignon)*

78

MAESTROPHONE MAESTRO soundbox. Made in Switzerland.

MAGIC NOTES. Trade mark of Columbia.

MAGNET. A German marque being marketed in London in 1906. (Fig. 204).

MAGNETOPHON. A tape recorder made by A.E.G., Berlin, in 1935.

MARATHON discs. Produced by the National Phonograph Company between 1912 and 1915. These were fine-groove phono-cut discs with a playing time of 16½mins.

MARCONI discs. Guglielmo Marconi was brought in by Columbia as technical adviser. In 1907, a record label carrying his name was introduced.

MARQUIS. A Leipzig-built instrument marketed in 1907 by the Polyphon Supply Company, London.

MAXITONE ELECTRIC. Marque of portable instrument. Probably of German manufacture.

MELBA. An instrument introduced by Gramophone & Typewriter Limited in 1905. Fitted with an Exhibition soundbox and Morning Glory horn as standard. See Specification 65.

MELBA records. Identified by mauve labels. Produced by Gramophone & Typewriter Limited and priced at one guinea.

MELOPHONE. A cheap instrument fitted with a Swiss-made Maestophone reproducer. See Specification 130. (Fig. 205).

MELOTONE. Disc label of the Brunswick Record Company, U.S.A.

MERVEILLEUX, LE. Made by Lioret c. 1900. Sold in Britain by Rowe & Company, London—the sole agents.

MICOTON. A heating apparatus sold to juke box owners to melt shellac for filling worn centre holes. (Fig. 206).

MIGNON. German marque marketed by M. & A. Wolfe, Fore Street, in 1912. Probably made by Carl Lindstrom of Berlin. See Specification 131.

MIGNON. Alternative name for Columbia Graphophone Model Q of 1901. (Figs. 207 and 208).

MIGNON. Paris. Makers of the Mignonphone camera-type instrument. See Specification 179. (Fig. 209).

MIKIPHONE. A miniature instrument in the form of a watch. Made in the 1920s by Vardasz Brothers. See Specification 180. (Fig. 210).

MIKKY PHONE. A Japanese-made miniature instrument. See Specification 181. (Fig. 211).

MONARCH. A Leipzig-built instrument marketed in 1907 by the Polyphon Supply Company, London.

MONARCH. Marketed by Gramophone & Typewriter Limited in 1901 and available at least up to 1912. Fitted with the Exhibition soundbox, and advertised with single, double and triple springs, and a variety of arms. See Specifications 56, 61, 62, 63 and 64. (Figs. 212, 213, 214, 215 and 216).

MORNING GLORY HORN. Introduced towards the end of 1904 by Gramophone & Typewriter Limited. Sold originally as an accessory, but fitted as standard on the 1905 Melba. Later supplied with all models.

209 Mignonphone

210 Mikiphone

210a Mikiphone—closed

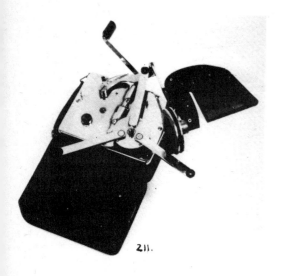

211.

213

212

214

215.

216

211 Mikki Phone

212-216 Variations of Gramophone Monarch Instruments

80

MURDOCH. London importer of instruments made by the German manufacturer, Excelsior, which were sold until 1911. Murdoch also marketed the Tournophone among other makes of instruments and records.

MUSIC MASTER HORN. Fitted to Triumph B in 1906.

MUSICRAFT CORPORATION, U.S.A. Recording studios.

N.P. See New Process.

NATIONAL GRAMOPHONE COMPANY, New York. Founded in 1896 by F. Seaman as an exclusive agency for Berliner gramophones.

NATIONAL PHONOGRAPH COMPANY. Founded by Thomas A. Edison in January 1896, making the Spring Motor (renamed the Triumph in 1900) and the Clockwork (renamed the Home) in that year. The company's European headquarters were established in Antwerp in 1897—these were moved to London in 1904. In 1902 there was an agreement between talking machine manufacturers, under which the National company were permitted to make only cylinders and cylinder playing instruments. This state of affairs lasted until 1912 and the introduction of the Edison Diamond Disc Phonograph and records.

217.

NEOPHONE records. Made from 1904 to 1908 by the Neophone Company, Finsbury Square, London. These were phono-cut records—the needle starting in the middle—comprising a white celluloid surface on a paper backing. 20ins discs with a playing time of 12mins were made.

NEW ORPHEUS. See Pathephone Orpheus.

NEW POLYPHON SUPPLY COMPANY, London. Sold the Symphony Monarch in 1909.

NEW PROCESS cylinders. Introduced by Edison Bell in 1908.

NIC SONORA. A Spanish-made combined film strip projector and talking machine. (Fig. 217).

NICOLE records. So-called 'indestructible' discs made in 1903. They were not popular and quickly disappeared from the market. They were made from a red coloured material.

NIER & EHMER, Saxony. Makers of Nirona instruments.

NIRONA. Trade name of Nier & Ehmer, Beirefeld, Saxony. See Specifications 66, 182, 199, 200. (Figs. 218, 219, 220, 221, 222 and 223).

218

NORTH AMERICAN PHONOGRAPH COMPANY. Founded in 1888 by financier, J. Lippincott, to commercially exploit both the phonograph of Edison and the gramophone of Bell and Tainter. Machines were not sold but hired to customers. The enterprise was not a success, and in 1893 was forced into liquidation by Edison in order for him to regain control of his patents. The company marketed what was probably the first commercially available cylinder recordings for $1 in the 1889-90 period. The company exported Edison products to Europe.

ODEON DISC MACHINE. Made in Germany from c.1904. See Specification 67.

211 Nic Sonora

218 Nirona

219-223 Variations of Nirona Instruments

224 Odeon No 50

82

ODEON NO. 50. Fitted with the Victory No. 4 soundbox. See Specification 183. (Fig. 224).

ODEON records. These were the first German-made discs to be sold in Britain. In 1904 Odeon produced the first double-sided discs. By 1913 the marque was under the control of Carl Lindstrom. See Instrument Specifications 133, 134, 135. (Figs. 225, 226 and 227).

ODEONETTE 244. See Specification 132. (Fig. 228).

O KEH PHONOGRAPH CORPORATION, New York. Recording studios, active in 1913.

OLYMP 21. A German coin-operated automat of 1910. (Fig. 229).

OPERA. Introduced by Edison's National Phonograph Company in 1912. Renamed the Concert. Along with other Edison external horn models, production ceased in 1913. See Specification 21. (Figs. 230, 231 and 232).

ORIGINAL STEIDINGERMOTORE, St Georgen, Black Forest. Make of motor fitted to Indufon 138 instrument.

ORPHONE. A public hall instrument marketed by Pathe in 1907, using compressed air for amplification.

OWEN, W. B. Came to England to represent Emile Berliner in 1897, and to establish the Gramophone Company with rights to sell gramophones and records throughout Europe.

PAILLARD, Switzerland. Makers of machines depending upon hot air. Their Apollo 10 ran for twelve hours on one charge of methylated spirit. Another instrument was the Model 205 Polyeucte. See Specification 68. (Figs. 232 and 234).

PANDORA. A German make of cylinder machine marketed in England in 1906. (Fig. 235).

PARKINS & GOTTO, Oxford Street, London. In 1891 the company advertised the Kammerer & Reinhardt-made Berliner gramophone at two guineas.

PARLAPHON AUTOMAT JUNIOR. A German-made instrument introduced in 1912. (Figs. 236 and 237).

PARLAPHON (PARLOPHONE). The trade name used by Carl Lindstrom of Berlin. See Specifications 69, 70, 136, 137. (Figs. 238, 239, 240 and 241).

PARR, Elias. English maker of the polyphon from c.1885, in collaboration with Paul Lochmann in Germany.

PARSONS, Sir Charles. By 1904, Parsons had developed an electrically-driven air compressor for increased volume—a process which had been invented and patented by Horace Short between 1898 and 1903. The device was marketed as the Auxetophone from 1905, by Gramophone & Typewriter Limited. (Fig. 242).

PATHE AIGLON. See Specification 33. (Fig. 243).

PATHE CONCERT MODEL A. Introduced c.1908. Marketed in 1910-11 as The Majestic. There was also a Concert-U. See Specifications 75, 144. (Figs. 244 and 245).

225.

226

225-226 Odeon Instruments

227

228.

229

230

231

232.

227 Odeon
228 Odeonette 244
229 Olymp. 21, 1910
230 Edison Opera
231 Edison Opera, 1912
232 Edison Opera Model A

233

234.

235

236.

237

238.

233 Apollo No 10, 1910
234 Paillard Model 205 Poleucte
235 Pandora, 1906
236 Parlaphon Automat, 1912
237-238 Parlaphon

85

239-241 Parlaphon Instruments

*242 Parson's Auxetophone by The Gramophone
Company, 1905*

243 Pathe Aiglon

244.

245.

246.

249.

247

248.

244 Pathe Concert A
245 Pathe Concert U
246-247 Pathe Coq
248 Pathe Duplex No 2
249 Pathe Elf

PATHE COQ. Sold from 1903 at £2 12s 6d. See Specifications 34, 35. (Figs. 246 and 247).

PATHE DUPLEX. NO. 2. Sold from c.1904 at £3 10s. See Specification 36. (Fig. 248).

PATHE ELF. Introduced in 1913 and listed at £1 17s 6d. See Specification 145. (Fig. 249).

PATHE FRERES, Paris. Pathe were recording operatic discs as early as 1896. A London office was established in 1903. The Pathe cylinders were made in 1906. Pathe's early discs were phono-cut discs for playing with a sapphire needle. they did not make needle-cut discs until 1921. See Specifications 31, 32, 71, 72, 73, 74, 88, 138, 139, 140, 141, 142, 143. (Figs. 250, 251, 252, 253, 254, 255, 256, 257, 258, 259, 260, 261 and 262).

PATHE LA JEUNESSE. Built c.1906. Later called 'No. 1'. See Specification 146. (Fig 263).

PATHE MODEL 0. DEMOCRATIC. The cheapest of the Pathe range. Available c.1903 to 1905 at £1 14s. See Specification 37. (Fig. 264).

PATHE MODEL B. Introduced c. 1906. See Specification 76. (Fig. 265).

PATHE REFLEX. Introduced 1912. See Specification 147. (Fig. 266).

PATHEPHONE MAJESTIC. A public hall instrument using compressed air for amplification. Designed to play 20ins discs. Introduced in 1909.

PATHEPHONE ORPHEUS. Also known as No. 36. Introduced in 1912. In 1913-14 the model was renamed the New Orpheus. See Specification 148.

PEROPHONE. An instrument of Continental origin. Marketed in London by Lockwood.

PETER PAN. A Swiss made instrument in the form of a camera, patented in Britain by E. A. Ferris. In 1923 it was sold by the Peter Pan Gramophone Limited of Gerrard Street and Frith Street, London. See Specifications 184, 185. (Figs. 267 and 268).

PHONAUTOGRAPH. Invented by Leon Scott de Martinville in 1857. It comprised a large horn terminating in a broad membrane connected to a stylus in contact with smoke-blackened paper wrapped around a cylinder. It was the basis for the Gramophone of Emile Berliner in 1887.

PHONDISC records. Made by Edison Bell from July 1908. There were two sizes: 12ins at 4s, and 8¾ins at 1s 6d.

PHONODIFF. A French or Swiss make. See Specification 186. (Fig. 269).

PHONOGRAPH. Popularly an overall term to describe cylinder playing machines. Originally it was the name given by Edison to his invention. In the U.S.A., the word *phonograph* is still used to describe all—and even modern—record playing machines.

PIDGEON, W. Maker of a copy of Edison's phonograph in collaboration with A. Stroh in 1878, for use in William Preece's demonstrations.

PIGMY GRAND. Introduced in 1909 by Gramophone & Typewriter Limited as the first of the company's portables. It was a table model without a lid.

250 Pathe Compressed Air Instrument, 1907

251 Pathe

252.

253

254

255.

256.

257.

252-257 Variations of Pathe Instruments

258

259

260

261.

262.

263.

258-262 Variations of Pathe Instruments

263 Pathe La Jeunesse No 1

264

265

266

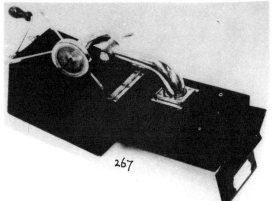

267

269

268.

264 *Pathe No 0 Democrat*
265 *Pathe Model B*
266 *Pathe Reflex*
267-268 *Peter Pan*
269 *Phonodiff*

270

271

In the following year, totally enclosed 'table grands' with lids were produced. See Specifications 119, 120. (Figs. 270, 271 and 272).

PIXIEPHONE. A toy machine. See Specification 201. (Fig. 273).

POLYDOR. German make. See Specification 187. (Fig. 274).

POLYEUCTE. See Paillard.

POLYPHONE. Made from c.1885 by Paul Lochmann (Germany) and Elias Parr (England).

POLYPHON COMPANY, Chicago. A subsidiary of the German company. In production at least until 1920. In 1898 the company produced an amplifier attachment with two soundboxes in tandem, each with its own horn.

POLYPHON MUSIKWERKE, Leipzig. Maker of Klingsor machines.

POLYPHON SUPPLY COMPANY, London. Imported German-made instruments, including the Leipzig produced Monarch, Baron, Marquis and Regina machines. See Specifications 77, 78.

POPULAR records. Made from 1898 by Edisonia Limited.

POULSEN, Valdemar. Patentee of a magnetic recorder in 1898. Production was undertaken by the American Telegraphone Company.

PREECE, Sir William. Chief Engineer to the G.P.O. in January 1878, when he read a newspaper article by Henry Edmunds, describing a demonstration of the Edison phonograph Edmunds had seen in the U.S.A. Impressed, Preece ordered a tinfoil phonograph to be made which he demonstrated at the Royal Institution.

PREMIER. An instrument made by Columbia. (Fig. 275).

PREMIER cylinders. Made by the Columbia Phonograph Company and intended for use on the Twentieth Century Premier Gramophone. Widely used from 1908 on Dictaphones.

PRESCOTT, F. M., New York. Appears as sole export agent on a surviving example of a c.1901 Zon-o-Phone.

PRETTNER, Germany. Known to have been in production in 1912.

PUCK. Made in Germany. The cheapest of all cylinder playing machines, selling for between 3s 6d and 5s. In the U.S.A., it was actually given away free with Columbia cylinders. The Puck is said to have been the invention of W. Bahre, and was made by a number of manufacturers, including Carl Lindstrom from about 1896, Lyra and Fritz Puppel. In 1905, a Puck instrument was introduced which could play both cylinder and disc records. (Figs. 276, 277, 278, 279 and 280).

PUPPEL, Fritz. German manufacturer of Puck type instruments, as well as other cylinder and disc machines. Known to have been in production in 1909. The London agent was A. Wolfe.

PYROLAPHON. An instrument believed to be of German origin. See Specification 149. (Fig. 281).

QUEEN ANNE. One of the seven styles of Gramophone Grand cabinets available in 1909.

270 *Gramophone Pigmy Grand, 1909*

271 *Gramophone Pigmy Grand*

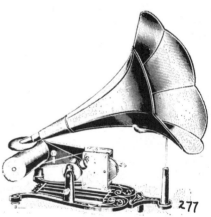

272 *Gramophone Pigmy Grand*

273 *Pixiephone*

274 *Polydor*

275 *Columbia Premier*

276 *Puck, early model*

277 *Puck Lyra, with flower horn, 1905*

278 Puck for Disc and Cylinder, 1905

279-280 Puck-type Instruments

281 Pyrolaphon

282 Radior

RADIO GRAMOPHONE MODEL 520. Produced by H.M.V.

RADIOR. An instrument with a Swiss-made motor. See Specification 150. (Fig. 282).

RALLY PORTABLE. Produced by Barnett Samuel & Sons, makers of Decca instruments. Model A was priced at £4 10s and Model B at £5 5s.

RECORDING ANGEL. The trade mark of the Gramophone Company in England and the Victor Company in the U.S.A., until gradually replaced by 'His Master's Voice' dog picture. The Angel has been re-introduced since World War II for use on a series of operatic Long Playing records.

RED GEM. Alternative name for the Gem Model D.

RED LABEL records. Produced by the Gramophone Company, selling at 10s.

REGINA. A Leipzig-built machine imported in Britain by the Polyphon Supply Company, London, c.1907.

RENA COMPANY. Selling double-sided discs for 2s 6d in 1909. The company was acquired by Columbia before that year.

REX cylinders. Introduced in the 1905-7 period.

RIESEN-LYRA. A German patented horn made by Clemens Humann. Advertised in 1910.

ROWE & COMPANY. 15 Aldermanbury, London, E.C. Agents for Lioret c.1901.

RUNGE & VON STEMANN. Germany. Makers of the Model 28—a Puck type instrument. See Specification 38. (Fig. 283).

RYSICK, A. C. Dresden. Maker of a coin-operated instrument from 1909. See Specification 39. (Fig. 284).

SAMUEL, Barnett. An old-established musical instrument dealer who turned his attention to talking machines in 1901, stocking most important makes, including Dulcephone, for which his company were sole agents. Introduced the Decca portable in 1913.

SATURN soundbox. A German production fitted to some camera type instruments.

SCHROEDER, Carl. Berlin. Makers in 1912-13 of the Excellent No. 51 instrument.

SCOTT DE MARTINVILLE, Leon. France. Inventor of the 1857 Phonautograph, a machine for translating sound waves into diagram form.

SEAMAN, F. Founder of the National Gramophone Company, New York, in 1896, marketing Berliner gramophones. Seaman abandoned Berliner interests in 1899 to organise the Universal Talking Machine Company, manufacturing the Zonophone under licence from the American Gramophone Company.

SENIOR MONARCH. Introduced by the Gramophone Company in 1905.

SHERATON. An elegant cabinet style introduced by Gramophone & Typewriter Limited in 1906, selling for £35. The instrument incorporated a 12ins turntable and speed indicator. This was one of seven styles of Gramophone Grand available in 1909.

283 Runge & Von Stemann No 28

284 A.C.R. Automat

SHORT, Horace. Inventor of an electrically driven compressor which forced air through vanes in the soundbox. Short, who was one of the founders of the Short Brothers aircraft works, carried on development of his invention from 1898 until 1903, when he sold the patent rights to Sir Charles Parsons, who improved it up to the point of manufacture by Gramophone & Typewriter Limited in 1906.

SONORA CORPORATION, U.S.A. Makers in the mid-1920s of the Sonora Melodie instrument. See Specification 151. (Fig. 285).

SOUNDMIRROR. A magnetic tape recorder for home use, produced by the Brush Development Company in 1947.

SPRANGOPHONE. A German-made machine with a telescopic tonearm. See Specification 188. (Fig. 286).

SPRING MOTOR PHONOGRAPH. Marketed by the National Phonograph Company in 1896, and renamed the Triumph in 1900. The instrument sold for $100 in its original form. (Fig. 287).

STANDARD. Models A, B, C, D, E, F, and G. The best known of Edison instruments. Introduced by the National Phonograph Company in 1898, it was made by Edison Bell in London from 1904. A more compact version was produced in the 1909-12 period, utilising some of the features of the Gem. See Specifications 22, 23, 24, 25. (Figs. 288, 289, 290, 291 and 292).

STARKTON records. Discs with a greater than normal groove pitch, intended for public hall use.

STENTORPHONE. Made by H. A. Gaydon. This was a public hall instrument, introduced in 1910, using compressed air for amplification. It was often used for the sound backing with early talking pictures. (Fig. 293).

STERLING records. Introduced in 1906, selling at 1s. Later that year, the cylinders were slightly increased in length. The label was bought by J. E. Hough in 1908, and continued to be marketed for a few years.

STERLING, (SIR) CHARLES. Came to England from the U.S.A. in 1903, to work with Gramophone & Typewriter Limited. He managed the British Zonophone Company for about a year, and in 1905 moved to the Russell Hunting Recording Company, making Sterling records until 1907. He was in charge of Rena record production until this marque was taken over by Columbia in 1909, after which he was appointed managing director of the British branch, and promoted to European general manager in 1914.

STILLE, Dr Kurt. Patentee of a design of tape recorder that was developed into the Blattnerphone.

STOLLWERK, Germany. In 1902 this company produced a toy instrument using a chocolate disc which could be eaten afterwards.

STROH, A. Built a model of a phonograph in collaboration with W. Pidgeon, for William Preece to use at lectures and demonstrations in 1878. (Figs. 294 and 295).

SYLVIA C. German make of cylinder machine marketed in London c.1906. (Fig. 296).

285 Sonora Melodie

286 Sprangophone

287.

288

289.

290

291

292.

287 Edison's Spring Motor Phonograph, 1895
288-289 Edison Standard Model A
290-291 Edison Standard Model B
292 Edison Standard Model D

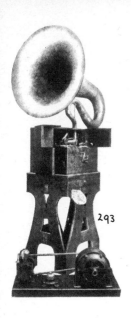

293 *Gaydon Stenorphone, 1914*

294 *Stroh's Modified Tinfoil Phonograph*

295 *Stroh's Mechanically-driven Phonograph*

296 *Sylvia C, 1906*

297-298 *Symphonion VII*

SYMPHONION NO. VII. Made c.1902. It resembled the Gramophone Company's Trade Mark model. See Specifications 80, 81. (Figs. 297 and 298).

SYMPHONY GRAND. See Columbia Symphony Grand.

SYMPHONY MONARCH. Advertised in 1908 by the New Polyphon Supply Company, London, at £2 10s. See Specification 82. (Fig. 299).

SYRENA. A cylinder-playing Puck instrument.

TAINTER, Charles Sumner (1854-1940). Worked with Alexander Graham Bell on the development of the telephone. With Christopher Bell, Tainter produced the graphophone in 1885.

TELEFUNKEN LIDO. An early instrument of this famous German manufacturer. See Specification 189. (Fig. 300).

TELEGRAPHONE. A magnetic recorder patented by Valdema Poulsen while employed by the Copenhagen Telephone Company in 1898. The instrument was demonstrated at the Paris Exposition of 1900.

TEMPOPHON. A talking machine mounted on a clock. Presumed to be of German origin. See Specification 152. (Fig. 301).

TERPOPHON. A miniature instrument, presumably of German origin. See Specification 190. (Fig. 302).

TOURNAPHONE. A German make of disc-playing instrument. Models A, H, K, and Baby Tournaphone were being marketed in London in 1906. (Figs. 303, 304 and 305).

TRIUMPH. Made in 1909 by Biedermann & Czarnikow, Berlin.

TRIUMPH. Models A, B, C, D, E, F, and G. The name Triumph was applied to the National Phonograph Company's Spring Motor instrument of 1900. It remained on the market with some modifications until 1912. The Triumph had a triple-spring motor and played 14 cylinders at one winding. See Specifications 26, 27. (Figs. 306, 307, 308, 309, 310 and 311).

TRIUMPHON. Made by Beidermann & Czarnikow, Berlin.

THORENS MON PIANO. Made in Switzerland, Thorens' trade mark is an anchor on a cross. See Specifications 153, 191, 192. (Figs. 312, 313 and 314).

THORENS soundbox. Fitted to instruments carrying 1914 patents. Some Thorens machines had Miraphone soundboxes.

TWIN records. Amalgamated with the British Zonophone Company in 1911.

TWOPHONE. Introduced in 1903 to play both cylinders and discs. The venture was not a success.

TYPE XP records. See High Speed records.

ULTONIA soundboxes. Patented 18 September 1917. Fitted to instruments built in the U.S.A. by the Brunswick-Balke-Collander Company.

ULTRAPHON. Made in the mid-1920s. See Specifications 154. 155, 156, 157, (Figs. 315, 316 and 317).

UNITED STATES GRAMOPHONE COMPANY, Washington, DC. Founded by Emile Berliner in 1893. The following year, the company produced the first electrically driven gramophone.

299

300

299 Symphony Monarch

300 Telefunken Lido

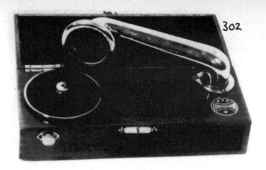

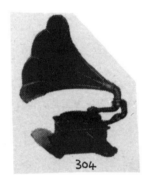

301 Tempophon

302 Tempophon

303 Baby Tournaphone, 1906

304 Tournaphone Model H, 1906

305 Tournaphone Model K, 1906

306

307

311

308

309

310

Variations of Edison Triumph Instruments

306 Model A

307 Model B

308 Model C/D

309 Model E/F/G

310 Model A

311 Model B

101

312

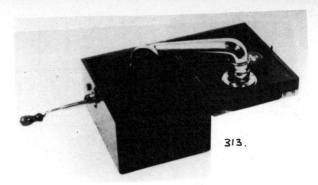

313.

315

314

316

317

312 Thorens Mon Piano

313-314 Variations of Thorens Instruments

315-317 Variations of Ultraphon Instruments

UNIVERSAL TALKING MACHINE COMPANY, U.S.A. Founded by F. Seaman in 1899, to manufacture the Zonophone under licence from the American Graphophone Company.

VARDASZ BROTHERS. Makers of miniature machines in the 1920s.

VELVET FACE records. Introduced in 1911 by J. E. Hough Limited. These needle-cut records were sold in two sizes: 12ins at 4s, and 10ins at 3s.

VICTOR. Made from 1899 by the Consolidated Talking Machine Company. The instrument was identical to Berliner's gramophone. From 1901 it was made by the Victor Talking Machine Company.

VICTOR MONARCH. Originally introduced by the Gramophone Company as the Victor in 1908. Being one of the machines in the company's Monarch series, it was logically renamed the Victor Monarch. See Specification 55. (Fig. 318).

VICTOR TALKING MACHINE COMPANY, Camden, New Jersey, U.S.A. Founded in 1901 as the successor to the Consolidated Talking Machine Company to build the Victor, a gramophone of Berliner's design.

VICTOR TRIPLEPHONE. A public hall instrument demonstrated in 1904 at Crystal Palace, to an audience of 20,000.

VICTOR VICTORIA. The name given to the Gramophone Grand of 1907 when sold in the U.S.A.

VICTOR V. Made in the U.S.A. from 1912. See Specification 83. (Fig. 319).

VICTORY NO. 4 soundbox, German make. Fitted to Odeon No. 50 instrument.

VOCOLION GRADUOLA. A record player fitted with remote volume control, using a Bowden cable from an armchair. It could open and close swell shutters in the horn mouth.

VOLTA GRAPHOPHONE COMPANY. Founded as the holding company for the patents of Bell and Tainter.

VOLTA LABORATORIES ASSOCIATION, Washington, DC. Founded by Alexander Graham Bell. Where the graphophone was developed between 1881 and 1885.

VOX. Germany. See Specifications 159, 160. (Figs. 320 and 321).

WHITE records. Introduced in England in 1905. In the following year the cylinders were slightly increased in length.

WINNER records. Introduced by J. E. Hough Limited in 1912. The selling price was 1s 6d.

WOLF, M. & A. Fore Street Avenue, London. Marketed the German-made Mignon machine from 1912. This instrument was probably built by Lindstrom in Berlin.

WOLFF, A. London agent for the German manufacturer, Fritz Puppel.

YOUNG, J. Lewis. 69 Fore Street, London, E.C. Importer of Edison instruments between 1891 and 1893.

318 Gramophone Victor Monarch

319 Victor V

320-321 Variations of Vox Instruments
322 Zonophon G.m.b.H. Resonanz Apparat
323 Zon-o-phon Standard

ZONOPHON GmbH. '*Resonaz Apparat*'. Probably made by Bumb & Konig c.1909. The Zonophon No. 16 was introduced in 1906. See Specification 161. (Fig. 322).

ZON-O-PHONE. Identical in principle to the gramophone of Berliner. It was made from 1899 by the Universal Talking Machine Company under licence from the American Graphophone Company, and in Germany by the Deutsche Grammophon Aktiengesellschaft. The model called 'The Standard' was made in the U.S.A. from c. 1901. F. M. Prescott, New York, appears as sole export agent on a surviving example. See Specifications 84, 86, 87. (Figs. 323 and 324).

ZONOPHONE CHAMPION. Built by the Gramophone Company in England from c.1910. See Specification 85. (Fig. 325).

324 Zon-o-phon Standard

325 Zonophon Champion

105

5. *Specifications of Production Instruments*

SPECIFICATIONS OF PRODUCTION INSTRUMENTS
  i **Cylinder playing instruments.**
 ii **Disc playing instruments with external horns.**
iii **Disc playing instruments with internal horns.**
 iv **Portable instruments.**
  v **Toy instruments.**

The following specifications must be regarded only as guidelines to the identification of instruments. Manufacturers were, as now, constantly changing their productions, both radically and in detail. Also, customers often fitted different horns and soundboxes of their choice. Consequently, it is very difficult to know if a surviving instrument is in the form its makers intended.

Cabinet, case and turntable sizes, with reference to the illustrations in the Directory of Marques, Inventors, and Manufacturers are, in the main, the best guides to identification.

i. CYLINDER PLAYING INSTRUMENTS

1. COLUMBIA GRAPHOPHONE TYPE A c.1898
   Case $11\frac{1}{2}$ x 7 x $10\frac{1}{2}$ins. Open spring motor. Curved slot winding handle. See also page 64.

2. COLUMBIA GRAPHOPHONE TYPE A
   Case $11\frac{1}{2}$ x 7 x $10\frac{1}{2}$ins. With Bettini reproducer and horn. See also page 64.

3. COLUMBIA GRAPHOPHONE TYPE AA c.1900
   Case $10\frac{1}{2}$ x $7\frac{1}{2}$ x $9\frac{1}{2}$ins. Double-spring ($\frac{5}{8}$ x 2ins dia barrel). Slotted end winding handle. See also page 64.

4. COLUMBIA GRAND TYPE AB c.1900—LATER CALLED DOUBLE EAGLE
   Base size 15 x $11\frac{1}{2}$ins. To play 5ins dia cylinders. Internal thread end winding handle. See also page 64.

5. COLUMBIA GRAPHOPHONE TYPE AT 1898
   Case $12\frac{1}{2}$ x $12\frac{1}{2}$ x $8\frac{1}{2}$ins. Internal thread end winding handle. See also page 64.

6. COLUMBIA GRAPHOPHONE TYPE BK (THE JEWEL)
   Case $12\frac{1}{2}$ x 8 x $6\frac{1}{2}$ins. Improved Lyric reproducer. Double-spring motor. Black japanned tin horn with brass bell, 7 x 14ins. Internal thread end winding handle. See also page 64.

7. COLUMBIA GRAPHOPHONE TYPE BX (THE EAGLE) 1899
   Base size $11\frac{1}{2}$ x 7ins. Height 6ins. Open spring motor. Black japanned horn 4 x 11ins. Internal thread end winding handle. See also page 64.

8. COLUMBIA GRAPHOPHONE TYPE E
   Case 14 x $8\frac{3}{4}$ x 12ins. Powered by 2 volt wet-cell battery. Plays $1\frac{1}{4}$ins dia.

cylinders. Edison cylinders may be played by using a sleeve. See also page 64.

9. EDISON BELL GEM 1904
Fitted with Model C reproducer. Plays 2min wax cylinders. It differs from the Edison Gem in that the carriage moves on a rod instead of a straight edge. See also page 52.

10. EDISON CLASS M PHONOGRAPH. Last patent date 1888
Case 19 x 9½ x 8¼ins. Electrically driven. DC current from wet-cell battery. Fitted with listening tubes. See also page 52.

11. EDISON CLASS S PHONOGRAPH 1893
Case 17½ x 10 x 6ins. Electrically driven. DC current from wet-cell battery. See also page 52.

12. EDISON CONCERT PHONOGRAPH 1899
Base size 16½ x 12ins. Height to top of mandrel 12¾ins. Plays 5ins dia cylinders. Triple-spring motor. Square internal hole wind handle. See also page 52.

13. EDISON FIRESIDE MODEL B 1909
To play 2min and 4min cylinders. Single-spring motor. Black japanned 'Cygnet' horn, 18½ x 25ins. Internal thread end winding handle. See also page 55.

14. EDISON GEM MODEL A 1901
Base size 7¾ x 5¾ins. Single-spring motor—⅝in spring. 10ins black japanned horn as standard. but often fitted with larger horn. Slotted end winding handle. See also page 55.

15. EDISON GEM MODEL C October 1907
Horn 11 x 20ins. Fixed handle. See also page 55.

16. EDISON GEM MODEL D (THE RED GEM)
Case 10 x 7¾ x 8ins. To play 2min and 4min cylinders. Horn 11 x 20ins. Fixed handle. See also page 55.

17. EDISON HOME MODEL A c.1898
Case 16½ x 8 x 12ins. Single-spring motor. Black japanning. Slotted end wind handle. See also page 69.

18. EDISON HOME MODEL A WITH 'NEW STYLE' CASE 1901
Case 18 x 9 x 12¼ ins. See also page 69.

19. EDISON HOME MODEL A WITH 'NEW STYLE' CASE (VARIATION)
Diamond B reproducer. Red flower horn, 23 x 30ins. See also page 69.

20. EDISON HOME MODEL B 1906
Case 16½ x 9 x 12¼ins. Motor mounted on underside of wooden frame. Blue flower horn, 19 x 24ins. Internal thread end wind handle. See also page 69.

21. EDISON OPERA MODEL A 1912
Case 18 x 12¾ x 14¾ins. To play 4min Blue Amberol cylinders. Metalwork finished in maroon enamel. Music Master horn, 21 x 22ins. Diamond A

reproducer. Internal thread end wind handle. See also page 83.

22. EDISON STANDARD MODEL A (TYPE 2 STANDARD) 1901-2

New style case 12¾ x 8¾ x 10¾ins. Model C reproducer for 2min cylinders only. Slotted end wind handle. See also page 96.

23. EDISON STANDARD MODEL B Late 1905

Case 13 x 9½ x 11¼ins. Single-spring motor. Horn 15 x 30ins. Internal thread end wind handle. See also page 96.

24. EDISON STANDARD MODEL B c.1907

Case 13 x 9½ x 11¾ins. Model C reproducer. Single-spring motor. Horn 7 x 14ins. Internal thread end wind handle. See also page 96.

25. EDISON STANDARD MODEL D

Case 13 x 9½ x 11¾ins. Single-spring motor. To play both 2min and 4min cylinders. Internal thread end wind handle. See also page 96.

26. EDISON TRIUMPH MODEL A c.1900

'New Style' case 18½ x 12¾ x 14½ins. Triple-spring motor. Internal thread end wind handle. See also page 99.

27. EDISON TRIUMPH MODEL B 1906

Case 18½ x 12¾ x 14½ins. Music Master horn, 22 x 36ins. Internal thread end wind handle. See also page 99.

28. EXCELSIOR 1906

Base 12½ x 9ins. Vertical wind handle—earlier models had horizontal wind handles. Belt-driven mandrel. Horn 15 x 14ins. Slotted end wind handle. See also page 55.

29. HARDY TINFOIL PHONOGRAPH 1878

Base 8½ x 9¾ins. Height to top of mandrel 5½ins. Mandrel 5½ins dia x 2ins. Mica or glass diaphragm. See also page 66.

30. LIORET LE MERVEILLEUX c.1900

Case 7½ x 4 x 4½ins. Small celluloid horn. See also page 74.

31. PATHE

Case 12½ x 8½ x 3¼ins. Orpheus attachment for larger horn and cylinders. Horn 13½ x 17ins. Slotted end wind handle. See also page 88.

32. PATHE

Case 10½ x 7 x 4¼ins. Orpheus attachment for larger horn and cylinders. Horn 11¾ x 14ins. Slotted end wind handle. See also page 88.

33. PATHE AIGLON

Case 11¾ x 8¾ x 8ins. To play 2min wax cylinders. Horn 10 x 27ins. Internal thread end wind handle. See also page 83.

34. PATHE COQ 1903

Case 12 x 7¾ x 6ins. To play 2min cylinders. Fitted with listening tubes. Internal thread end wind handle. See also page 88.

35. PATHE COQ

Case 13½ x 9¼ x 7ins. Fitted with Orpheus attachment to use larger horn and/ or sleeve to play 3½ins dia Salon size cylinders. Standard horn 15½ x 18ins. Slotted end wind handle. See also page 88.

36. PATHE DUPLEX NO. 2 1904-5
   Case 12 x 8¾ x 10ins. Fitted with Orpheus attachment to play 3½ins dia Salon size cylinders. Slotted end wind handle. See also page 88.

37. PATHE NO. 0 DEMOCRAT 1903
   Case 9½ x 6¾ x 5½ins. Belt drive from single-spring motor. Horn 10¼ x 13½ ins. Internal thread end wind handle. See also page 88.

38. RUNGE & VON STEMANN NO. 28 c.1903
   Base size 8 x 6 x 4ins. Horn 7 x 12ins. Internal thread end wind key. See also page 95.

ii DISC PLAYING INSTRUMENTS WITH EXTERNAL HORNS

39. A.C.R. AUTOMAT 1909
   Case 15 x 15 x 8½ins. Slot takes 10 pfg coins. 9¾ins. turntable. Horn 23 x 26 ins painted red, yellow and black. See also page 95.

40. AUXETOPHONE
   Case 31 x 18 x 41½ins. Electric motor forces air through vanes in soundbox. Triple-spring motor. 12ins dia turntable. Gooseneck tonearm. See also page 36.

41. BERLINER HANDCRANKED GRAMOPHONE. Early 1890s
   Base size 12 x 6ins. 5ins turntable. Papier mache horn. Carbon diaphragm. See also page 37.

42. BERLINER HAND-CRANKED GRAMOPHONE 1894
   Base size 13¾ x 6¼ins. Brass horn, 3 x 9ins. Mica diaphragm soundbox. See also page 37.

43. BERLINER HAND-CRANKED GRAMOPHONE. February 1895
   Base size 16 x 9ins. 7ins turntable. Brass horn 5¼ x 13½ins. (Later—1897— models thought to have black japanned horn). See also page 37.

44. CONCERT AUTOMATIQUE FRANCAIS
   Case 21 x 21 x 44ins. Pathe soundbox. Coin operated. Double-spring motor with 4½ins spring barrel. 11ins turntable. 25ins dia horn. Curved slot wind handle. See also page 46.

45. DETECTIVE DISC RECORDING MACHINE 1892
   Box 14½ x 8 x 7ins. Slow speed (20min 5ins dia wax discs). Key winding. Horn 3½ x 18ins. See also page 14.

46. GRAMOPHONE c.1902.
   Horn 9¾ x 15ins. Slotted-end wind handle. See also page 64.

47. GRAMOPHONE. CAPTAIN SCOTT'S SENIOR MONARCH
   Case 13½ x 13½ x 7ins. Triple-spring motor. 12ins dia turntable. Exhibition soundbox. Internal thread end wind handle.

48. GRAMOPHONE. JUNIOR MONARCH. Late 1904
   Case 11 x 11 x 5¾ins. Single-spring motor. Nickel horn 12 x 18ins. 10ins turntable. Exhibition soundbox. Slotted-end wind handle. See also page 71.

49. GRAMOPHONE. JUNIOR MONARCH. Late 1908
   Case 11¼ x 11¼ x 6ins. 10ins turntable. Wood-grained metal horn (probably

German) 18 x 19ins. Exhibition soundbox. Slotted-end wind handle. See also page 71.

50. GRAMOPHONE. Lumiere CABINET GRAND No. 510
Quadruple-spring (1¼ins) motor. External thread end wind handle. See also page 77.

51. GRAMOPHONE. Lumiere COMBINED GRAMOPHONE AND WIRELESS
Case 20¼ x 14½ x 17ins. Double-spring motor. 12ins dia turntable. External thread end wind handle. Fitted with 2 valve crystal set. See also page 77.

52. GRAMOPHONE. Lumiere No. 460. July 1924
Case 17¼ x 22½ x 11ins. Double-spring (1¼ins) motor. 14ins dia diaphragm. 12ins turntable. External thread end wind handle. See also page 77.

53. GRAMOPHONE MODEL No. 2 1898
Base size 10 x 8ins. Vertical handcrank handle. Japanned tin horn (straight) 5 x 15ins. Clark-Johnson soundbox. See also page 61.

54. GRAMOPHONE MODEL 5 (HEO) 1913
Case 14¾ x 14¾ x 6½ins. Double-spring motor with two 3¼ x 1¼ins barrels. Exhibition soundbox. Internal thread end wind handle.

55. GRAMOPHONE. VICTOR MONARCH. Late 1908
Case 10¾ x 11 x 5ins. 10ins turntable. Black petal horn 15 x 18ins. Exhibition soundbox. Single-spring motor. Slotted end wind handle. See also page 103.

56. GRAMOPHONE. MONARCH c. 1910
Case 14¾ x 14¾ x 7ins. Double-spring motor with 4 x 1¼ins barrel. 10ins turntable. See also page 79.

57. GRAMOPHONE. MONARCH JUNIOR. October 1902
Case 10 x 10 x 3¼ins. Base 13ins square. Single-spring motor. Brass horn 11½ x 18ins. 10ins turntable. See also page 71.

58. GRAMOPHONE No. 7 1910
Case 17 x 17 x 17½ins. 12ins turntable. Exhibition soundbox. 21 x 24ins horn. External thread end wind handle. See also page 61.

59. GRAMOPHONE No. 7 Late 1910
Case 17 x 17 x 7ins. Triple-spring motor. 12ins turntable. Internal thread end wind handle. See also page 61.

60. GRAMOPHONE TYPE II (INTERMEDIATE MONARCH) 1910
Case 13½ x 13½ x 6½ins. Medium taper tonearm. 10ins turntable. Single-spring motor. Exhibition soundbox. Black metal flower horn, 16 x 18ins. Internal thread end wind handle. See also page 71.

61. GRAMOPHONE & TYPEWRITER MONARCH Early 1903
Case 12 x 12 x 7ins. Single-spring motor. 10ins turntable. Nickel plated brass horn 15 x 22ins. Exhibition soundbox. Slotted end wind handle. See also page 79.

62. GRAMOPHONE & TYPEWRITER MONARCH Early 1903
Case 13 x 13 x 6½ins. Otherwise as 61. See also page 79.

63. GRAMOPHONE & TYPEWRITER MONARCH. February 1904

Case 12 x 12 x 7ins. Gooseneck folding tonearm. Single-spring motor. Horn 16 x 27ins. Internal thread end wind handle. See also page 79.

64. GRAMOPHONE & TYPEWRITER MONARCH 1904-1909

Case 12 x 12 x 6½ins. Single-spring motor. 3½ x 1ins barrel. Brass horn, 16 x 24ins. Exhibition soundbox. Curved slot end wind handle. See also page 79.

65. MELBA GRAMOPHONE 1905

Case 13 x 13 x 7½ins. Gold plated fittings. Triple-spring motor. 12ins turntable. H.M.V. Exhibition soundbox. Horn 18 x 20ins. Internal thread end wind handle. See also page 79.

66. NIRONA

Case 12 x 12 x 6ins. 10ins turntable. Single-spring motor. Slotted end wind handle. See also page 81.

67. ODEON DISC MACHINE c.1904

Case 12 x 12 x 7ins. Nickel plated horn 6½ x 10ins. Odeon IT soundbox with 1½ins mica diaphragm. 10½ins turntable. Internal spigot wind handle. See also page 81.

68. PAILLARD MODEL 205 POLYEUCTE

Case 20 x 19 x 12ins. Hot air powered. Horn 25½ x 28½ins. 12½ins turntable. See also page 83.

69. PARLAPHON

Case 13 x 13 x 5½ins. Green horn 18 x 22ins. Straight tonearm. Parola soundbox with 2ins mica diaphragm. 10ins turntable. Internal spigot wind handle. See also page 83.

70. PARLAPHON

Case 16½ x 16½ x 7ins. Straight tonearm. Soundbox with 1⅞ins mica diaphragm. Single-spring motor, 4 x 1¼ins barrel. 11¾ins turntable. Heavy gauge brass horn 17½ x 30ins. Internal thread end wind handle. See also page 83.

71. PATHE

Case 17 x 17 x 8½ins. Wooden flower horn 23 x 24ins. Double-spring motor. Soundbox with 2ins mica diaphragm. 12ins turntable. Curved slot end wind handle. See also page 83.

72. PATHE

Case 16½ x 16½ x 9¼ins. Black metal horn 24 x 28ins. Single-spring motor, 3¼ x 1½ins barrel. 11ins turntable. Soundbox with 2½ins mica diaphragm. Slot end wind handle. See also page 88.

73. PATHE c. 1908

Case 10¾ x 10¾ x 4¾ins. Red horn 13 x 12ins. 7¾ins turntable. Slotted end wind handle. See also page 88.

74. PATHE c.1908

Case 14½ x 14½ x 6¾ins. Pale blue horn, 17½ x 21½ins. Single-spring motor, 3½ x 1⅞ins barrel. Pathe Ebonite soundbox with 2ins mica diaphragm. 9½ins turntable. Slotted end wind handle. See also page 88.

75. PATHE CONCERT A c.1909
  Case 17 x 17 x 8½ins. Flower horn 24 x 29ins. Single-spring motor, 3¾ x 1¾ ins barrel. Pathe soundbox with 2⅜ins mica diaphragm. 11¼ins turntable. To play 20ins discs. Slotted end wind handle. See also page 83.

76. PATHE MODEL B c.1900
  Case 11½ x 11½ x 7½ins. Soundbox with aluminium diaphragm. Single-spring motor. 9¾ins turntable. Horn 11½ x 17ins. Slotted end wind handle. See also page 88.

77. POLYPHON c.1909
  Case 18 x 18 x 8½ins. Soundbox with 2ins mica diaphragm. Gooseneck tapered tonearm. 12ins turntable. Blue and maroon horn, 26 x 28ins. Curved slot wind handle. See also page 92.

78. POLYPHON No. 1492 (still in production 1920)
  Case 16 x 16 x 9¾ins. Ural double-spring motor. Brown and red metal horn 26ins dia. 11¾ins turntable. No. 23 Expression soundbox. Slotted end wind handle. See also page 92.

79. RONEOPHONE by PATHE FRERES 1909
  Recording machine 17½ x 13 x 12ins. Base of record shaving machine 14 x 14 x 5½ins. For 7 x ½ins thick discs. Horn 3 x 12ins.

80. SYMPHONION No. VII c.1902
  Box 8¼ x 8¼ x 4½ins. Nickel plated horn. Parola soundbox with 1½ins mica diaphragm (but may not be original). 7ins turntable. Slotted end wind handle. See also page 99.

81. SYMPHONION 1903
  Case 11½ x 11½ x 4½ins. 10ins turntable. Black horn 11½ x 17ins. See also page 99.

82. SYMPHONY MONARCH 1908
  Case 9ins dia x 4½ins. Green horn 13 x 14ins. 8ins turntable. Soundbox with 1¾ins mica diaphragm. Slotted end wind handle. See also page 99.

83. VICTOR V 1912
  Case 16 x 16 x 7½ins. Triple-spring motor 3 x 1¼ins. Dark red metal horn 23 x 24ins. Exhibition soundbox with gooseneck tonearm. 12ins turntable. Slotted end wind handle. See also page 103.

84. ZONOPHONE No. 16 Late 1904
  Case 8¼ x 7 x 4½ins on plinth. 7ins turntable. Perfect soundbox. Nickel horn 10 x 16ins. Internal spigot wind handle. See also page 105.

85. ZONOPHONE CHAMPION c.1910
  Case 12 x 12 x 6½ins. Brass horn 22 x 24ins. Double-spring motor. 10ins turntable. Internal thread end wind handle. See also page 105.

86. ZON-O-PHONE STANDARD c.1901
  7ins turntable. Single-spring motor. Internal spigot wind handle. See also page 105.

87. ZON-O-PHONE 1901
  Nickel horn. Internal spigot wind handle. See also page 105.

iii DISC PLAYING INSTRUMENTS WITH INTERNAL HORNS

88. PATHE (OPTIONAL INTERNAL AND EXTERNAL HORN)

Case 17 x 17 x 8½ins. Internal horn 8 x 6ins. Single-spring motor. External horn 19 x 20ins. 11½ins turntable. Slotted end wind handle. See also page 88.

89. AMBEROLA VI

Case 16¾ x 22 x 15½ins. Diamond Model B reproducer. See also page 35.

89A. AMBEROLA 30

Case 12½ x 16 x 12¾ins. Diamond Model C reproducer. Single-spring motor driving the mandrel directly by gears. External thread end wind handle. See also page 35.

90. AMBEROLA 50

Case 15½ x 15 x 19¾ins. Diamond Model C reproducer. Double-spring motor driving mandrel through gears. External thread end wind handle. See also page 35.

91. AMBEROLA 91

Case 15 x 19 x 41ins. Other details as Amberola 50. See also page 35.

92. BRUNSWICK MODEL 200 (Registration date 13 Feb. 1923)

Case 18½ x 20 x 43ins. 12ins turntable. Ultona soundbox (Pat. Sept. 1917) may be turned to play lateral or vertical cut records. Internal thread end wind handle. See also page 40.

93. BRUNSWICK TABLE MODEL 105 c.1921

Case 19½ x 17 x 15ins. 11¾ins turntable. Soundbox has two needle holes and may be turned to play lateral or vertical cut records. External thread end wind handle. See also page 40.

94. COLUMBIA GRAFONOLA 22A. Mid-1920s

Case 14½ x 18½ x 21½ins. Triple-spring Garrard motor. External thread end wind handle. See also page 58.

95. COLUMBIA GRAFONOLA 25A Mid-1920s

Case 39½ x 18 x 19½ins. Triple-spring Garrard motor. 12ins turntable. Columbia No. 7 soundbox. External thread end wind handle. See also page 58.

96. DECCA 'DECCALION' Late 1920s

Case 42 x 22 x 23ins. 12ins turntable. Curved slot end wind handle. See also page 46.

97. DEUTSCHE GRAMMOPHON

Piano shaped case 55 x 31 x 37ins. 12ins turntable. Slotted end wind handle. See also page 50.

98. EDISON CHIPPENDALE CONSOLE c.1909

Case 40 x 22½ x 37ins. 10½ins turntable. External thread end handle. See also page 40.

99. EDISON DIAMOND DISC PHONOGRAPH MODEL C200 1912-13

Case 19½ x 19½ x 46ins. Metal internal horn. Some models had gold plated soundbox. Single-spring motor, 4½ x 1¾ins barrel. External thread end wind handle. See also page 52.

100. EDISON LONDON (L 35) c.1927
   Case $17\frac{1}{2}$ x $20\frac{1}{2}$ x 19ins (overall height 46ins). To play both standard and long playing Edison Diamond Discs. $11\frac{1}{2}$ins turntable. See also page 77.
101. EDISON LONDON CONSOLE (LC 38)
   Cabinet 34 x $20\frac{1}{2}$ x 34ins. To play Edison Diamond Discs. External thread end wind handle. See also page 77.
102. EDISON LONDON No. 1 (L 35)
   Case 18 x $19\frac{3}{4}$ x 19ins (overall height 44ins.) $11\frac{1}{2}$ins turntable. External thread end wind handle. See also page 77.
103. GETRAPHON
   Case 10 x 10 x 4ins. Single-spring motor. $5\frac{3}{4}$ins turntable. Small gooseneck tonearm. Soundbox (Swiss-made Maestrophone Maestro) with $1\frac{7}{8}$ins mica diaphragm. Internal thread end wind handle. See also page 55.
104. GILBERT Late 1920s
   Case 22 x 20 x 30ins. 12ins turntable. 'Gilbert Tone Reflector' soundbox, aluminium diaphragm, with mother-of-pearl facings. Bugle-shaped tonearm. External thread end wind handle. See also page 55.
105. GRAMOPHONE CABINET GRAND No. 180 1923
   Case 43 x 21 x $22\frac{3}{4}$ins. $1\frac{3}{4}$ins quadruple-spring motor. 12ins turntable. External thread end wind handle. Originally fitted with No. 2 soundbox, later with No. 4. See also page 58.
106. GRAMOPHONE HORNLESS MODEL No. 1 1914-15
   Case $14\frac{1}{2}$ x $14\frac{1}{2}$ x $6\frac{3}{4}$ins. Single-spring motor. 10ins turntable. Exhibition soundbox. Internal thread end wind handle (later models had external thread end wind handle). See page 58.
107. GRAMOPHONE HORNLESS MODEL No. 3 16 April 1913
   Case 17 x 17 x 9ins. Double-spring motor. 12ins turntable Exhibition soundbox. Internal thread end wind handle. See also page 58.
108. GRAMOPHONE HORNLESS MODEL NO.60 December 1922.
   Case $15\frac{1}{4}$ x $16\frac{1}{2}$ x 9ins. Double-spring $1\frac{1}{4}$ins motor. Exhibition soundbox. 12ins turntable. External thread end wind handle. See also page 58.
109. GRAMOPHONE JUNIOR GRAND (German version) c.1909
   Double-spring motor. Gooseneck tonearm. See also page 71.
110. GRAMOPHONE LIBRARY BIJOU GRAND 1909
   Case $17\frac{3}{4}$ x $25\frac{1}{4}$ x 46ins. Triple-spring motor. 12ins turntable. Exhibition soundbox. Internal thread end wind handle. See also page 61.
111. GRAMOPHONE MODEL 12 (called CZ when exported) 1910
   Case 20 x $23\frac{1}{2}$ x 19ins. Double-spring motor. 12ins turntable. Exhibition soundbox. Slotted end wind handle. See also page 61.
112. GRAMOPHONE MODEL 109 1925
   Case 15 x $18\frac{1}{4}$ x $13\frac{1}{4}$ins. Double-spring motor. Curved goosneck tonearm. No. 4 soundbox. 10ins turntable. External thread end wind handle. See also page 61.
113. GRAMOPHONE MODEL 125 December 1922

Case 17 x 20½ x 14½ins. Double-spring 1¼ins motor. 12ins turntable. No. 2 soundbox. External thread end wind handle. See also page 61.

114. GRAMOPHONE MODEL 130 1929
Case 18 x 17¼ x 13¾ ins. Double-spring motor. No. 5A soundbox with alloy diaphragm. 12ins. turntable. See also page 61.

115. GRAMOPHONE MODEL 157 UPRIGHT GRAND
Case 36¼ x 18¼ x 20ins. No. 5A soundbox. 12ins turntable. External thread end wind handle. See also page 61.

116. GRAMOPHONE MODEL 163 1927
Case 39¾ x 22 x 21½ins. No. 5A soundbox. 12ins turntable. External thread end wind handle. See also page 61.

117. GRAMOPHONE MODEL 265 October 1922
Case 37½ x 38¼ x 28¼ins. Quadruple-spring motor. No. 2 soundbox. 12ins turntable. Gold plated fittings. External thread end wind handle. See also page 61.

118. GRAMOPHONE MODEL 461 1926
No. 4 soundbox. Double-spring motor. 12ins turntable. External thread end wind handle. See also page 61.

119. GRAMOPHONE PIGMY GRAND 1909
Case 15 x 12¾ x 7½ins. Gooseneck tapering tonearm. Single-spring and double-spring models available. Internal thread end wind handle. See page 92.

120. GRAMOPHONE PIGMY GRAND
Case 15¼ x 13¼ x 7½ins (there are other models). Exhibition soundbox. Internal thread end wind handle. See also page 92.

121. GRAMOPHONE UPRIGHT GRAND No. 202 1927
Case 49½ x 23½ x 28½ins. 12ins turntable. No. 5B soundbox with alloy diaphragm. Re-entrant exponential horn. 'Matched impedance' system developed by Westinghouse Electric. External thread end wind handle. See also page 64.

122. H.M.V. AUTOMATIC GRAMOPHONE No. 12 June 1930
Case 28¼ x 23½ x 41¾ins. 8¾ins turntable. 11¾ins No. 7B straight pick-up arm. See also page 66.

123 H.M.V. ELECTRIC REPRODUCER No. 551 1929
Case 24½ x 20 x 38¼ins. No. 7 pick-up head. Narrow gooseneck tonearm. See also page 66.

124. H.M.V. TABLE GRAND No. 109 1925
Case 18½ x 12½ x 15½ins. Otherwise as Gramophone Model 109. See also page 69.

125. HYMNOPHON c.1912
Case 12 x 12 x 7½ins. 9¾ins turntable. Slotted end wind handle. See also page 69.

126. KLINGSOR COIN-OPERATED INSTRUMENT
9½ins turntable. Slotted end wind handle. See also page 74.

127. KLINGSOR TABLE MODEL
Case 16 x 16 x 12ins. 10ins turntable. Mica diaphragm soundbox. Slotted end wind handle. See also page 74.

128. KLINGSOR VERDI 1912
Case 14½ x 14 x 30ins. Curved slot end wind handle. See also page 74.

129. KLINGSOR (NOVELTY MACHINE WITH DANCERS)
Case 15 x 14 x 38ins. Slotted end wind handle. See also page 74.

130. MELOPHONE
Case 12 x 11¼ x 3¼ins. Gooseneck tonearm. Horn with 4½ x 3¾ins aperture. Single-spring motor. 10ins turntable. Slotted end wind handle. Maestrophone reproducer with mica diaphragm. See also page 79.

131. MIGNON c.1912
Case 10 x 9 x 5¾ins. Single-spring motor, 2¾ins barrel. 6¾ins turntable. Mignon mica diaphragm soundbox. Slotted end wind handle. See also page 79.

132. ODEONETTE 244
Case 18 x 15 x 22ins. Curved gooseneck tonearm. Odeon Grand soundbox with 2ins mica diaphragm. 12ins turntable. See also page 83.

133. ODEON HORNLESS c.1914
Case 15 x 15 x 7½ins. 10¾ins turntable. Odeon Grand soundbox with mica diaphragm. Slotted end wind handle. See also page 83.

134. ODEON TABLE MODEL c.1912
Case 18 x 17 x 14ins. 10ins turntable. Odeon Grand with 2ins mica diaphragm. 'Flamingo' gooseneck tonearm. Slotted end wind handle. See also page 83.

135. ODEON TABLE MODEL c.1912
Case 14 x 14 x 13ins. 10ins turntable. Odeon Grand soundbox with 2ins mica diaphragm. Beka 'Flamingo' gooseneck tonearm. Internal spigot wind handle. See also page 83.

136. PARLAPHON
Case 20 x 16½ x 15ins. 11¼ins turntable. Curved slot end wind handle. See also page 83.

137. PARLAPHON 1913
Parlaphon Reform soundbox with 1½ins mica diaphragm. Single-spring motor. 9¾ins turntable. See also page 83.

138. PATHE
Case 18½ x 18½ x 16ins. Soundbox with 2ins mica diaphragm. 11ins turntable. Slotted end wind handle. See also page 88.

139. PATHE
Case 16 x 19 x 14ins. 9½ins turntable. Slotted end wind handle. See also page 88.

140. PATHE
Case 18½ x 18½ x 10ins. 9¾ins turntable. Pathe Concert soundbox with 2½ins mica diaphragm. Slotted end wind handle. See also page 88.

141. PATHE

Case 16 x 18 x 12ins. Single-spring motor. Oval internal horn mouth 7½ x 6ins. Soundbox with 2ins mica diaphragm. Slotted end wind handle. See also page 88.

142. PATHE

Case 18 x 25 x 15½ins. 11ins turntable. Soundbox with 2ins diaphragm. Curved slot end wind handle. See also page 88.

143. PATHE

Case 15 x 15 x 15ins. Pathe Concert soundbox. 9½ins turntable. Slotted end wind handle. See also page 88.

144. PATHE CONCERT U. c.1908

Case 27½ x 25½ x 36ins. Bell of horn, 21ins. 11¼ins turntable. To play 20ins discs. Slotted end wind handle. See also page 83.

145. PATHE ELF 1913

Case 14 x 14 x 11½ins. Pathe Ebonite soundbox. 8½ins turntable. Slotted end wind handle. See also page 88.

146. PATHE LA JEUNESSE 1906

Case 10 x 10 x 9ins. 6ins turntable. Thin metal horn. Slotted end wind handle. See page 88.

147. PATHE REFLEX

Case 17 x 17 x 14ins. 9½ins turntable. Slotted end wind handle. See also page 88.

148. PATHEPHONE 36 ORPHEUS 1912

Case 20½ x 19 x 13ins. 9¾ins turntable. Pathe Concert soundbox with 2½ins mica diaphragm. Slotted end wind handle. See also page 88.

149. PYROLAPHON

Case 14 x 14 x 12ins. 9¾ins turntable. Slotted end wind handle. See also page 92.

150. RADIOR

Case 15 x 12 x 4½ins. 7ins tonearm. Diamond soundbox to play vertical-cut records. Swiss-made motor. 8ins turntable. Slotted end wind handle. See also page 95.

151. SONORA MELODIE. Mid-1920s.

Case 17 x 17 x 14ins. 12ins turntable. Entire sound conduit in multiple wood. Internal thread end wind handle. See also page 96.

152. TEMPOPHON

Case 12 x 14 x 7½ins. 6ins turntable. Incorporating a clock. Could be set to play at a preselected time. Two soundboxes, for lateral and vertical cut records. See also page 99.

153. THORENS MON PHONO

Case 10½ x 8½ x 4½ins. 5½ins turntable. Single-spring motor, 2½ins barrel. Curved slot end wind handle. See also page 99.

154. ULTRAPHON

Case 17ins dia x 12ins. Two tonearms (reason obscure). 9¼ins turntable. See also page 99.

155. ULTRAPHON. Mid-1920s.

Case 20ins dia x 15ins. 12ins turntable. Slotted end wind handle. See also page 99.

156. ULTRAPHON

Case 21ins dia x 21ins. Electrically driven motor. Two wooden tonearms with 2ins mica diaphragms. 12ins turntable. See also page 99.

157. ULTRAPHON

Case 21ins dia x 40ins. 11½ins turntable. Two metal tonearms with 2ins mica diaphragms. Slotted end wind handle. See also page 99.

158. VICTROLA VV—IX c.1922

Case 17 x 14 x 19½ins. Double-spring motor, 3 x 1¼ins barrel. Victrola No. 2 soundbox with 1½ins mica diaphragm. External thread end wind handle.

159. VOX

Case 22 x 17¼ x 19½ins. 12ins turntable. Wooden soundbox with 2ins mica diaphragm. Grubu 10S Double-spring motor 3 x 1ins barrel. Internal thread end wind handle. See also page 103.

160. VOX

Case 20 x 19½ x 15ins. 12ins turntable. Slotted end wind handle. See also page 103.

161. ZONOPHON GmbH RESONANZ APPARAT c.1909

Case 19½ x 17 x 13ins. 9¾ins turntable. Slotted end wind handle. See also page 105

iv **PORTABLE INSTRUMENTS**

162. ACUSTON

Case 11 x 10 x 5½ins. Soundbox with 2ins mica diaphragm. Curved 2-part tonearm. 6ins turntable. Slotted end wind handle. See also page 35.

163. ADLER

Case 7 x 4 x 7ins. Slotted end wind handle. See also page 35.

164. BIEDERMANN & CZARNIKOW TRUMF

Case 10¾ x 8½ x 5ins. 5¼ins turntable. Soundbox with mica diaphragm. External thread end wind handle. See also page 37.

165. CAMERAPHONE c.1925

Case 4½ x 6¼ x 5¼ins. With 'tortoise shell' hemispherical horn. Slotted end wind handle. See also page 40.

166. COLUMBIA 100 1930.

Case 12 x 8½ x 5ins. Soundbox with alloy diaphragm. Gooseneck tonearm. 7¾ins turntable. See also page 40.

167. COLUMBIA 202 1929.

Case 16 x 11¾ x 6½ins. Automatic brake. Gooseneck tonearm with 'phono-reflex' shapings. Metal diaphragm soundbox. 9¾ins turntable. Wind handle fixed but folding. See also page 40.

168. CRYSTALPHONE

Case 9 x 6 x 7ins. 1¾ins turntable with retaining nut to hold disc. U.S. made 'Jewel' soundbox for playing vertical and lateral cut records. Slotted end wind handle. See also page 46.

169. DECCA JUNIOR PORTABLE STYLE JC (dated 24 October 1925).

Case 9½ x 8¼ x 10¾ins. 8ins turntable. Soundbox with 1⅞ins mica diaphragm. Internal thread end wind handle. See also page 50.

170. DECCA MODEL XL (dated 24 January 1928).

Case 9¼ x 12 x 6¾ins. 8ins turntable. Telesmatic soundbox with 2ins mica diaphragm. External thread end wind handle. See also page 50.

171. DECCA SALON MODEL 130 c.1929

Case 16½ x 11½ x 7½ins. Metal diaphragm soundbox. 9¾ins turntable. External thread end wind handle. See also page 50.

172. EXCELDA

Case 11 x 4½ x 2ins. Tapering 7ins tonearm. Soundbox with alloy diaphragm. See also page 54.

173. EXCELLENCE

Case 14 x 1½ x 4¾ins. 7ins nickel plated turntable—record supported on 5 felt pads. External thread end wind handle. See also page 54.

174. H.M.V. No. 101 1928

Case 11¼ x 16¼ x 5¾ins. No. 4 soundbox. Single-spring motor. 10ins turntable. External thread end wind handle. See also page 69.

175. H.M.V. No. 102 1929

Case 11¼ x 6¼ x 5¾ins. No. 4 soundbox. Single-spring motor. 10ins turntable. Spline end wind handle. See also page 69.

176. HYMNOPHON PORTABLE

Case 11½ x 11½ x 7¼ins. 9¼ins turntable. Slotted end wind handle. See also page 69.

177. LIORET MODEL C c.1900

Hunting type horn, made in 3 pieces. Internal thread end key. See also page 74.

178. LIORETGRAPH NO. 2 1900

Mica diaphragm reproducer flared to form horn See also page 74.

179. MIGNONPHONE

Camera type case 8¾ x 5¼ x 2¾ins. Collapsible cardboard horn covered with pale green cloth. Octagonal Mignon (Paris) soundbox. To play vertical or lateral cut discs. 4⅜ins turntable. See also page 79.

180. MIKIPHONE (Latest British Patent Date 7 December 1925).

Case 4ins dia. Fixed key winder. See also page 79.

181. MIKKY PHONE

Case 5¾ x 4½ x 3¾ins. Flat horn on tonearm. Curved slot end wind handle. See also page 79.

182. NIRONA
Case 14 x 11 x 6ins. 8ins turntable. 6½ins tonearm. Soundbox with 2ins mica diaphragm. Slotted end wind handle. See also page 81.

183. ODEON NO. 50
Case 12 x 16 x 6ins. Gooseneck tonearm. 9¾ins turntable. Victory No. 4 alloy diaphragm soundbox. Spline end wind handle. See also page 83.

184. PETER PAN
Camera type case 7 x 4½ x 6ins. Collapsible horn. 4½ins turntable. Peter Pan soundbox with mica diaphragm. Slotted end wind handle. See also page 88.

185. PETER PAN
Case 4 x 6¼ x 5ins. Telescopic nickel horn. Curved slot end wind handle. See also page 88.

186. PHONODIFF
Case 11 x 15 x 8¼ins. 9¼ins turntable. External thread end wind handle. See also page 88.

187. POLYDOR
Case 10¼ x 11¼ x 7¾ins. 6¼ins turntable. Curved gooseneck tonearm. Slotted end wind handle. See also page 92.

188. SPRANGOPHONE
Case 6¼ x 5 x 7¼ins. Telescopic tonearm. 4¼ins turntable. Slotted end wind handle. See also page 96.

189. TELEFUNKEN LIDO
Case 12 x 14 x 6ins. 10ins turntable. Soundbox with 2¼ins mica diaphragm. External thread end wind handle. See also page 99.

190. TEROPHON
Case 9¾ x 4 x 3½ins. 3¼ins turntable. 6½ins soundarm. See also page 99.

191. THORENS
Case 8¼ x 6 x 4ins. Thorens 4½ins soundbox with alloy diaphragm. 6½ins tonearm. Curved slot end wind handle. See also page 99.

192. THORENS
Case 8⅜ x 6½ x 5½ins. 4¾ins turntable. Miraphone soundbox with mica diaphragm. Curved slot end wind handle. See also page 99.

v. TOY INSTRUMENTS

193. BING
Tinbox 6 x 6 x 3¾ins. Metal diaphragm. Black japanned horn, 2½ x 5ins. Push-on wind key. See also page 37.

194. BING PIGMYPHONE
Case 6½ x 6½ x 2¾ins. Alloy soundbox with metal diaphragm. 5¾ins turntable. Black japanned horn, 2½ x 5ins. Push-on key. See also page 37.

195. BINGOLA
Tin body 6 x 8 x 2½ins. 5¾ins turntable. Soundbox with mica diaphragm. Internal square push-on wind key. See also page 37.

196. BINGOLA

Plywood body 6¾ins across front tapering to 2¾ins at back, 8¾ins long. 6ins turntable. Soundbox with mica diaphragm. Internal thread end wind handle. See also page 37.

197. INDUPHON 138

Tin body 9¾ins dia. Single-spring motor, 2 x ¾ins barrel. 1⅝ins mica diaphragm soundbox. Curved slot end wind handle. See also page 69.

198. LEMIPHONE

Tin case 6ins dia x 2½ins. 5ins turntable. Tin horn 2¼ x 5ins. Internal square push-on key. See also page 74.

199. NIRONA 1920s

Tin case 8 x 8 x 4¾ins. 5⅞ins turntable. Soundbox with mica diaphragm. Slotted end wind handle. See also page 81.

200. NIRONA 1924.

Case 7ins dia x 4ins. Soundbox with mica diaphragm. Curved slot end wind handle. See also page 81.

201. PIXIEPHONE.

Peardrop shaped case 8 x 5ins. 5½ins turntable. Soundbox with mica diaphragm. Push-on wind key. See also page 92.

The Melba Gramophone of 1905. One of the most beautiful instruments ever manufactured.

Appendix I Family Tree of Companies with Roots in the U.S.A.

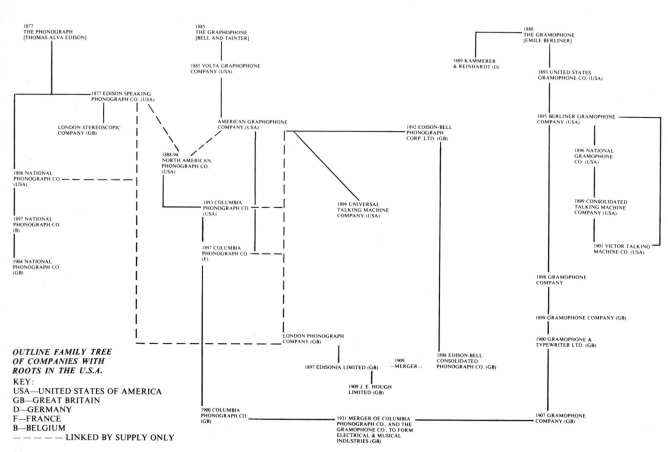

1877
THE PHONOGRAPH
[THOMAS ALVA EDISON]

1885
THE GRAPHOPHONE
[BELL AND TAINTER]

1888
THE GRAMOPHONE
[EMILE BERLINER]

1889 KAMMERER
& REINHARDT (D)

1885 VOLTA GRAPHOPHONE
COMPANY (USA)

1893 UNITED STATES
GRAMOPHONE CO. (USA)

1877 EDISON SPEAKING
PHONOGRAPH CO. (USA)

AMERICAN GRAPHOPHONE
COMPANY (USA)

1892 EDISON-BELL
PHONOGRAPH
CORP. LTD. (GB)

1895 BERLINER GRAMOPHONE
COMPANY (USA)

LONDON STEREOSCOPIC
COMPANY (GB)

1888-94
NORTH AMERICAN,
PHONOGRAPH CO.
(USA)

1896 NATIONAL
GRAMOPHONE
CO. (USA)

1896 NATIONAL
PHONOGRAPH CO.
(USA)

1893 COLUMBIA
PHONOGRAPH CO.
(USA)

1899 UNIVERSAL
TALKING MACHINE
COMPANY (USA)

1899 CONSOLIDATED
TALKING MACHINE
COMPANY (USA)

1897 NATIONAL
PHONOGRAPH CO.
(B)

1897 COLUMBIA
PHONOGRAPH CO.
(F)

1901 VICTOR TALKING
MACHINE CO. (USA)

1904 NATIONAL
PHONOGRAPH CO.
(GB)

1898 GRAMOPHONE
COMPANY

1899 GRAMOPHONE COMPANY (GB)

LONDON PHONOGRAPH
COMPANY (GB)

1900 GRAMOPHONE &
TYPEWRITER LTD. (GB)

OUTLINE FAMILY TREE OF COMPANIES WITH ROOTS IN THE U.S.A.

KEY:
USA—UNITED STATES OF AMERICA
GB—GREAT BRITAIN
D—GERMANY
F—FRANCE
B—BELGIUM
— — — — — LINKED BY SUPPLY ONLY

1897 EDISONIA LIMITED (GB)

1909
—MERGER—

1898 EDISON-BELL
CONSOLIDATED
PHONOGRAPH CO. (GB)

1909 J. E. HOUGH
LIMITED (GB)

1900 COLUMBIA
PHONOGRAPH CO.
(GB)

1931 MERGER OF COLUMBIA
PHONOGRAPH CO., AND THE
GRAMOPHONE CO., TO FORM
ELECTRICAL & MUSICAL
INDUSTRIES (GB)

1907 GRAMOPHONE
COMPANY (GB)

122

Appendix II Some Manufacturers' Literature

The "Rally" Portable (Model B) is fitted with the New "Crescendo" Sound Box, Swan-neck Tone Arm, and "Hall Mark" Worm Gear Motor and 10-inch Turntable. The circular metal deflector and the tonearm are carried on a moveable panel, which, by a most ingenious arrangement. rises and falls automatically as the lid is raised or lowered. Tonearm and soundbox are held in position by their own weight—not even a spring clip is needed—and the "Rally" is ready to play immediately opened. Moreover as a result of clever designing all moving parts are protected from all possibility of damage. The "Rally Portable" is entirely British, every part being made in the manufacturers' own or associated factories in England. It is strongly made, very compact and light, and so shallow that when not in use it may be put under the settee or in a cupboard, or anywhere.

For the home where it can be played in any room in the house the "Rally Portable" is a constant source of pleasure. It is always ready to play, always handy to entertain you and your friends, at your will and where you will. Out-of-doors it is even more desirable, for it is so extremely portable that it may be taken anywhere ; and another advantage is that it does not look like a gramophone, it looks just an ordinary well-made carrying case. The picnic of a few hours, the day on the river, the holiday in the Country or at the Seaside—all these are suitable occasions for the " Rally Portable." Let it be one of the party every time !

And now go to a Music Dealer or to the Gramophone Department of one of the Stores and ask to see and to hear the " Rally Portable." Note how well it is made, how subtly contrived. Then take hold of it and realise its lightness. And, finally, listen to it. Hear a string orchestra, a violin solo, a rousing rollicking song. How natural is the tone, how magnificent the volume, how clear the reproduction ! Truly the " Rally Portable " is as musical as it is portable.

Then why not have one in your own possession, at your service whenever you desire entertaining.

MODEL B   £5 5 0

The outer casing is of brown compressed grained fibre and has a nickel-plated attache lock and a patent "everlasting" carrying handle.

Single spring, worm gear motor (fitted with dial speed indicator and 10 in. turntable) playing 10 in. and 12 in. records. The nickel-plated tapering tone arm ("swan neck" pattern) is pivoted on to an embossed metal panel (copper-oxidized) which also serves as a sound deflector. The equipment of this "Rally" includes a "Crescendo" sound box with insulated rubber neck and 200 English steel needles of the best quality.

MODEL A £4 10 0

The outer casing is of crocodile - grained leather-cloth and has a pair of nickel-plated clasps and a patent "everlasting" carrying handle.

Single spring motor (fitted with dial speed indicator and 10 in. turntable) playing 10 in. and 12 in. records.

The nickel-plated tapering tone arm ("swan neck" pattern) is pivoted on to an embossed metal panel (copper-oxidized) which also serves as a sound deflector. The equipment of this " Rally " includes a " Hall Mark" Concert sound box and 200 English steel needles of the best quality.

SOLE MANUFACTURERS :
BARNETT SAMUEL & SONS. LTD., 32–36. Worthip St., London, E.C.2.

SOLF MANUFACTURERS :
BARNETT SAMUEL & SONS. LTD., 32–36, Worship St., London. E.C.2.

"She shall have music wherever she goes"

The "DECCA" Dulcephone

"Portable" - - "Powerful"

THE gramophone continues to grow in popularity; it is now-a-days no longer regarded merely as an amusement for a winter's evening, but as a constant and indispensable companion. Even a summer holiday without the familiar gramophone has something lacking, whilst almost any form of out-of-door recreation can be gladdened by its music.

Good gramophones—with ringing sonorous tone—are generally bulky and difficult to move about. Portable gramophones there have been, but relatively large and heavy ones, requiring carrying cases, etc., and—most important—having admittedly a weakened tone.

The "Decca" Dulcephone overcomes all earlier obstacles and is indisputably the gramophone "par excellence" for travelling, for out-of-doors—and for indoors as well. It really is portable and compact, and it astonishes with its loud pure tone.

Portability

It will be seen from the illustrations that the "Decca" Dulcephone is made like an ordinary handbag. It can thus be carried about without attracting notice and with the greatest of ease—it weighs approximately but 13 lbs.

Compactness

The "Decca" Dulcephone is entirely self-contained. Its case proper holds all the works and no outer cover is needed. Every bit of mechanism fits into the smallest space possible, but without any corresponding reduction in the volume of sound. The "Decca" has a full round tone of great richness. Moreover, it has no complicated parts, no adjusting is needed, and as soon as opened it is ready to play.

Tone

There is no mystery about the extraordinary volume of sound that issues from the "Decca" Dulcephone. Everyone knows the principle of deflection, *i.e.*, that a travelling force gathers impetus the moment it is deflected from another body. The "Decca" is the outcome of an ingenious application of this principle—its tone arm propels the sound waves into a hollow (inside the lid) whence they are deflected back again with greatly increased power.

Style 1 closed

Style 2 closed

STYLE 1. (£2 2 0)

Black grained Leatherette Case
(11½ ins. sq. by 10½ ins. high)

Swiss Motor playing one 12 in.
disc

" Duretta " Sound-Box. Metal
" Dulciflex " (black enamelled)

STYLE 2. (£3 3 0)

Brown Compressed Fibre Case,
with two spring locks
(10¾ ins. sq. by 10½ ins. high)
Swiss Motor (worm gear), playing two 10 in. discs, speed in-
dicating dial
" Crescendo " Sound - Box.
Polished Aluminium "Dulciflex " (spun in one piece)

UP THE RIVER.
Whether the inclination is to loll lazily
among the cushions, or energetically to ply
punt-pole or sculls . . . Music will enhance
the day's enjoyment The " Decca " Dulcephone
is an ever-ready never-failing source of Melody
(It is here pictured ready to be closed.)

125

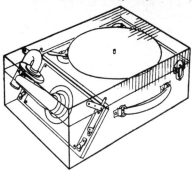

Weight : 11 lbs.
Size : 15 in. × 11 in. × 5½ in. high.

"X-Rayed." If you could just remove the casing this is how the "Rally" internal construction would appear.

THE PICNIC.
The welcome-meal—the well-earned rest—and the "Decca" Dulcephone. These are the three vital factors that go to make the perfect picnic. (The above picture shows the "Decca" open and ready to play.)

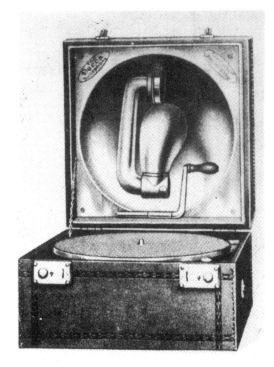

126

Style 3 ready to play

STYLE 3.   (£5 5 0)

Polished Cowhide Case (lea-
ther-lined), with two spring
locks
(10¾ ins. sq. by 10½ ins. high)
Double - spring Swiss Motor
(worm-gear) playing 3-4 10 in.
discs
"Crescendo - Major" Sound-
Box. Polished Aluminium
"Dulciflex" (spun in one
piece)

AT THE SEASIDE.

Music on the Sands . . . and the children (to say nothing
of the grown-ups) will extract every ounce of pleasure
from the yearly holiday. Unlike all other seaside entertainers, the "Decca" Dulcephone plays you the music
of your choice whenever and wherever you please
and it does not afterwards "come round with the hat."

Acknowledgements

The author and publishers acknowledge with gratitude the co-operation of Mr Leonard Petts, Electrical and Musical Industries Limited, and The Decca Gramophone Company Limited, for their ready advice and provision of pictorial matter.

Bibliography

CAIN, John. *TALKING MACHINES* (1961).
CHEW, V. K. *TALKING MACHINES* (1967).
THE E.M.I. COLLECTION catalogue.
GELATT, Roland. *THE FABULOUS PHONOGRAPH* (1956).
READ, Oliver and WELCH, Walter L. *FROM TIN FOIL TO STEREO* (1959).